The Secret of Power

Robert Collier

TABLE OF CONTENTS

INTRODUCTION

WHAT IS THE strongest political trend in the world today?

After the last war, it was towards democracy. But somehow democracy failed the average man. When the depression came and he found himself unable to provide food and shelter for his loved ones, he demanded something more than equality of opportunity. He demanded SECURITY from want.

To answer that demand came "Strong Men," so-called Mussolinis and Hitlers and Antonescus and Francos and the like, and Fascism was born. Men achieved security, of a kind, but they bartered their freedom for it. And soon they learned that power feeds on power, and the only end of dictatorship is war, which destroys all.

And the reason? The same reason that has impelled man since time began—the longing for security, security for the home, security against want, security for old age.

Since time began, the search for security has been one of the strongest urges in all of nature. You see it in the animal in the way it conceals its nest and tries to make it safe from predatory creatures—man or animal. You see it in the records of early man in the caves he dug into the sides of the mountains, in the tree huts, in the cliff dwellings. You follow it down through the ages to the walled cities, the turreted castles, the inaccessible mountains in which men made their homes.

Throughout history, you see this search for security as one of the dominant characteristics of all human kind. And now that the common man has realized his power, you find him all over the world banding together to take over all property, to the end that he and his may find that security from want that he has so long worked for.

What he does not seem to realize is that the mere redistribution of property never has and never will solve his problem. It will provide him with temporary supply, yes—but supply is a continuing problem, and when his small share of the general distribution is gone, he will be worse off than he was before, because production will have either ceased or been greatly curtailed.

Redistribution is not the answer. It has been tried repeatedly, and always failed. You must go farther back than that. You must start with the source of things. And that is what we shall try to do in the following pages.

"Know this, ye restless denizens of earth,
Know this, ye seekers after joy and mirth,
Three things there are, eternal in their worth—
LOVE, that outreaches to the humblest things;
WORK, that is glad in what it does and brings;
And FAITH, that soars upon unwearied wings.
Divine the powers that on this trio wait,
Supreme their conquest, over time and fate.
LOVE, WORK and FAITH, these three alone are great.

CHAPTER 1

THE CREATIVE FORCE

By the word of the Lord were the heavens made... (Psalm 33)

What is a word? A mental concept or image, is it not? In originating language, words were coined to represent certain images or objects. The word horse, for instance, calls to mind the image left upon the retina and the brain by what one has seen of that quadruped.

But what if there were no horses? What if one were called upon to create a horse, with no previous knowledge of such an animal? You'd have to build up a clear mental image of it first, would you not? You'd have to work out a mental picture of every part of its anatomy, every physical outline. You'd need a perfect mental concept of everything that is comprised in the word horse.

And that was what happened when God created the world. In the beginning was the "Word," the mental concept, the image in God's mind of what He planned. "And the Word was made flesh." It took on shape and substance. It grew into a habitable world. It developed creatures like the fish in the sea, the birds in the air, the beasts of the field. And finally man.

Life then, as now, was a continually developing process. Those early forms of life were threatened by every kind of danger—from floods, from earthquakes, from droughts, from desert heat, from glacial cold, from volcanic eruptions—but each new danger was merely an incentive to finding some new resource, to putting forth their Creative Force in some new shape.

To meet one set of needs, the Creative Force formed the Dinosaur; to meet another, the Butterfly. Long before it worked up to man, we see its unlimited resourcefulness in a thousand ways. To escape danger in the water, some forms of Life sought land. Pursued on land, they took to the air. To breathe in the sea, the Creative Force developed gills. Stranded on land, it perfected lungs. To meet one kind of danger, it grew a shell. For another, it developed fleetness of foot, or wings that carried it into the air. To protect itself from glacial cold, it grew fur; in temperate climes, hair. Subject to alternate heat and cold, it produced feathers. But ever, from the beginning, it showed its power to meet every changing condition, *to answer every creature's need.*

Had it been possible to stamp out this Creative Force, or halt its constant upward development, it would have perished ages ago, when fire and flood, drought and famine followed each other in quick succession. But obstacles, misfortunes, cataclysms, were to it merely new opportunities to assert its power. In fact, it required difficulties or obstacles to stir it up, to make it show its energy and resourcefulness.

The great reptiles, the monster beasts of antiquity, passed on as the conditions changed that had made them possible, but the Creative Force stayed, changing as each age changed, always developing, always improving.

When God put this Creative Force into His creatures, He gave to it unlimited energy, unlimited resource. No other power can equal it. No force can defeat it. No obstacle can hold it back. All through the history of life and mankind, you can see its directing intelligence rising to meet every need of life.

No one can follow it down through the ages without realizing that the purpose of existence is GROWTH, DEVELOPMENT. Life is dynamic, not static. It is ever moving forward—not standing still. The one unpardonable sin in all of nature is to stand still, to stagnate. The Gigantosaurus, that was over a hundred feet long and as big as a house; the Tyrannosaurus, that had the strength of a locomotive and was the last word in frightfulness; the Pterodactyl or Flying Dragon—all the giant monsters of pre-historic ages—are gone. They ceased to serve a useful purpose. They stood still while the life around them passed them by.

Egypt and Persia, Greece and Rome, all the great empires of antiquity, perished when they ceased to grow. China built a wall around herself and stood still for a thousand years. In all of Nature, to cease to grow is to perish.

It is for men and women who are not ready to stand still, who refuse to cease to grow, that this hook is written. Its purpose is to give you a clearer understanding of your own potentialities, to show you how to work with and take advantage of the infinite energy and power of the Creative Force working through you.

The terror of the man at the crossways, not knowing which way to turn, should be no terror for you, for your future is of your own making. The only law of infinite energy is the law of supply. The Creative Principle is your principle. To survive, to win through, to triumphantly surmount all obstacles has been its everyday practice since the beginning of time. It is no less resourceful now than it ever was. You have but to supply the urge to work in harmony with it, to get from it anything you need. For if this Creative Force is so strong in the lowest forms of animal life that it can develop a shell or a poison to meet a need; if it can teach the bird to circle and dart, to balance and fly; if it can grow a new limb on a spider or crab to replace a lost one; how much more can it do for YOU —a reasoning, rational being, with a mind able to work with this Creative Force, with energy and purpose and initiative to urge it on!

The evidence of this is all about you. Take up some violent form of exercise, and in the beginning your muscles are weak, easily tired. But keep on a few days, and what happens? The Creative Force in you promptly strengthens them, toughens them, to meet their need.

All through your daily life, you find this Force steadily at work. Embrace it, work with it, take it to your heart, and there is nothing you cannot do. The mere fact that you have obstacles to overcome is in your favor, for when there is nothing to be done, when things run along too smoothly, the Creative Force seems to sleep. It is when you need it, when you call upon it urgently, that it is most on the job.

It differs from Luck in this, that fortune is a fickle jade who smiles most on those who need her least. Stake your last penny on the turn of a card—have nothing between you and ruin but the spin of a wheel or the speed of a horse—and the chances are a hundred to one that luck will desert you.

It is just the opposite with the Creative Force in you. As long as things run smoothly, as long as life flows along like a song, this Creative Force seems to slumber, secure in the knowledge that your affairs can take care of themselves. But let things start going wrong, let ruin or death stare you in the face—then is the time this Creative Force will assert itself if you but give it the chance.

There is a Napoleonic feeling of power that insures success in the knowledge that this invincible Creative Force is behind your every act. Knowing that you have with you a force which never yet has failed in anything it has undertaken, you can go ahead in the confident knowledge that it will not fail in your case. The ingenuity which overcame every obstacle in making you what you are, is not likely to fall short when you have immediate need for it. It is the reserve strength of the athlete, the second wind of the runner, the power that, in moments of great stress or excitement, you unconsciously call upon to do the deeds which you ever after look upon as superhuman.

But they are in no wise superhuman. They are merely beyond the capacity of your conscious self. Ally your conscious self with that sleeping giant within you, rouse him daily to the task and those superhuman deeds will become your ordinary, everyday accomplishments.

10

It matters not whether you are banker or lawyer, businessman or clerk, whether you are the custodian of millions or have to struggle for your daily bread. The Creative Force makes no distinction between high and low, rich and poor. The greater your need, the more readily will it respond to your call. Wherever there is an unusual task, wherever there is poverty or hardship or sickness or despair, there this Servant of your mind waits, ready and willing to help, asking only that you call upon him. And not only is it ready and willing, but it is always ABLE to help. Its ingenuity and resource are without limit. It is mind. It is thought. It is the telepathy that carries messages without the spoken or written word. It is the sixth sense that warns you of unseen dangers. No matter how stupendous and complicated, or how simple your problem may be, the solution of it is somewhere in mind, in thought. And since the solution does exist, this mental giant can find it for you. It can know, and It can do, every right thing. Whatever it is necessary for you to know, whatever it is necessary for you to do, you can know and you can do if you will but seek the help of this Genie-of-your-mind and work with It in the right way.

To every living creature, God gave enough of this Creative Force to enable it to develop whatever it felt that it needed for survival. Behind and working through every living thing was this Creative Force, and to each was given the power to draw upon it at need. With the lower forms of life, that call had to be restricted to themselves, to their own bodies. They could not change their environment.

They could develop a house of shell in which to live, like the crustaceans or the snail or the turtle. They could use the Creative Force to develop strength or fleetness or teeth and claws—anything within or pertaining to themselves. But aside from building nests or caves or other more or less secure homes, they could not alter conditions around them. To man alone was given the power to make his own environment. To him alone was given dominion over things and conditions.

That he exercises this power, even today, only to a limited extent, does not alter the fact that he has it. Man was given dominion. "And God said—Let us make man in our image, after our likeness, and let them have dominion over the fish of the sea, and over the fowl of the air, and over the cattle, and over all the earth, and over every creeping thing that creepeth upon the earth."

Of course, few believe in that dominion. Fewer still exercise it for their own good or the good of all. But everyone uses the Creative Force in them to an extent. Everyone builds their own environment.

"Don't tell me," some will say indignantly, "that I built these slums around me, that I am responsible for the wretched conditions under which I work, that I had anything to do with the squalor and poverty in which my family have to live." Yet that is exactly what we do tell you. If you were born in poverty and misery, it was because your parents imaged these as something forced upon them, something they could not help, a condition that was necessary and to be expected. Thinking so, they used the Creative Force working through them to fasten those conditions upon themselves as something they were meant to suffer and could do nothing about.

Then you in your turn accepted those conditions as what you were born to, and fastened them upon yourself by your supine acceptance of them, by failing to claim better ones, by making no great or sustained efforts to get out of them.

All history shows that the determined soul who refuses to accept poverty or lack can change these to riches and power if they have the determination and the perseverance. The great men of the world have almost all come up from poverty and obscurity. The rich men of the world have mostly started with nothing.

"Always the real leaders of men, the real kings, have come up from the common people," wrote Dr. Frank Crane. "The finest flowers in the human flora grow in the woods pasture and not in the hothouse; no privileged class, no royal house, no carefully selected stock produced a Leonardo or a Michelangelo in art, a Shakespeare or Burns in letters, a Mozart or Paderewski in music, a Socrates or Kant in philosophy, an Edison or Pasteur in science, a Wesley or a Knox in religion."

It is the NEED that calls forth such geniuses, the urgent need for development or expression, and it is because these men drew powerfully upon the Creative Force within them that they became great.

"Look within," said Marcus Aurelius. "Within is the fountain of all good. Such a fountain, where springing waters can never fail, do thou dig still deeper and deeper."

God gave to man, and to man alone, the power to make his own environment. He can determine for himself what he needs for survival, and if he holds to that thought with determination, he can draw whatever is necessary from the Creative Force working through him to make it manifest. First the Word, the mental image, then the creation or manifestation.

Professor Michael Pupin says—"Science finds that everything is a continually developing process." In other words, creation is still going on, all around you. Use your Creative Force to create the conditions you desire rather than those you fear. The life about you is constantly in a state of flux. All you have to do is create the mental mold in which you want the Creative Force to take form, and then hold to that mold with persistence and determination until the Creative Force in it becomes manifest.

Dr. Titus Bull, the famous neurologist, says—"Matter is spirit at a lower rate of vibration. When a patient is cured, it is spirit in the cell doing the healing according to its own inherent pattern. No doctor ever cured a patient. All a doctor can do is to make it possible for the patient to heal themselves."

And if that is true of the body, it is just as true of conditions around you. Matter—physical materials—is spirit or Creative Force at a lower rate of vibration. The spirit or Creative Force is all around you. You are constantly forming it into mental molds, but more often than not these are dictated by your fears rather than your desires. Why not determinedly form only good molds? Why not insist upon the things you want? It is just as easy, and it works just as surely. Writes Emerson:

"There is no great and no small,
To the soul that maketh all;
And where it cometh, all things are;
And it cometh everywhere.

I am the owner of the sphere,
Of the seven stars and the solar year,
Of Caesar's hand, and Plato's brain,
Of Lord's heart, and Shakespeare's strain."

"Give me a base of support," said Archimedes, "and with a lever I will move the world."

And the base of support is that all started with mind. In the beginning was nothing—a fire mist. Before anything could come of it there had to be an idea, a mental model on which to build. *The God Mind* supplied that idea, that model. Therefore the primal cause is mind. Everything must start with an idea. Every event, every condition, every thing is first an idea in the mind of someone.

Before you start to build a house, you draw up a plan of it. You make an exact blueprint of that plan, and your house takes shape in accordance with your blueprint. Every material object takes form in the same way. Mind draws the plan. Thought forms the blueprint, well drawn or badly done as your thoughts are clear or vague. It all goes back to the one cause. The creative principle of the universe is mind, and thought forms the molds in which its eternal energy takes shape.

But just as the effect you get from electricity depends upon the mechanism to which the power is attached, so the effects you get from mind depend upon the way you use it. We are all of us dynamos. The power is there— unlimited power. But we've got to connect it with something—set it some task—give it work to do— else are we no better off than the animals.

The "Seven Wonders of the World" were built by men with few of the opportunities or facilities that are available to you. They conceived these gigantic projects first in their own minds, pictured them so vividly that the Creative Force working through them came to their aid and helped them to overcome obstacles that most of us would regard as insurmountable. Imagine building the Pyramid of Gizeh, enormous stone upon enormous stone, with nothing but bare hands. Imagine the labor, the sweat, the heartbreaking toll of erecting the Colossus of Rhodes, between whose legs a ship could pass! Yet men built these wonders, in a day when tools were of the crudest and machinery was undreamed of, by using the unlimited power of the Creative Force.

That Creative Force is in *you,* working through you, but it must have a model on which to work. It must have thoughts to supply the molds. There are in Universal Mind ideas for millions of wonders greater far than the "Seven Wonders of the World." And those ideas are just as available to you as they were to the artisans of old, as they were to Michelangelo when he built St. Peter's in Rome, as they were to the architect who conceived the Empire State Building, or the engineer who planned the Hell Gate Bridge.

Every condition, every experience of life is the result of our mental attitude. We can only do what we think we can do. We can be only what we think we can be. We can have only what we think we can have. What we do, what we are, what we have, all depend upon what we think. There is only one limit upon the Creative Force, and that is the limit we impose upon it.

We can never express anything that we do not first believe in. The secret of all power all success, all riches, is in first thinking powerful thoughts, successful thoughts, thoughts of wealth, of supply. We must build them in our own mind first. As Edgar A. Guest so well expressed it:

"You can do as much as you think you can, But you'll never accomplish more; If you're afraid of yourself, young man, There's little for you in store.

For failure comes from the inside first, It's there if we only knew it, And you can win, though you face the worst, If you feel that you're going to do it."

William James, the famous psychologist, said that the greatest discovery in a hundred years was the discovery of the power of the subconscious mind. It is the greatest discovery of all time. It is the discovery that man has within himself the power to control his surroundings, that he is not at the mercy of chance or luck, that he is the arbiter of his own fortunes, that he can carve out his own destiny. He is the master of the Creative Force working through him. As James Allen puts it:

"Dream lofty dreams, and as you dream, so shall you become. Your vision is the promise of what you shall one day be; your Ideal is the prophecy of what you shall at last unveil."

For matter is in the ultimate but a product of thought, the result of the mold into which you have put the Creative Force working through you. Even the most material scientists admit that matter is not what it appears to be. According to physics, matter (be it the human body or a log of wood—it makes no difference which) is made up of an aggregation of distinct minute particles called atoms. Considered individually, these atoms are so small that they can be seen only with the aid of a powerful microscope, if at all.

Until comparatively recent years, these atoms were supposed to be the ultimate theory regarding matter. We ourselves—and all the material world around us—were supposed to consist of these infinitesimal particles of matter, so small that they could not be seen or weighed or smelled or touched individually—but still particles of matter *and indestructible.*

Now, however, these atoms have been further analyzed, and physicists tell us that they are not indestructible at all—that they are mere positive and negative buttons of force or energy called protons and electrons, without hardness, without density, without solidity, without even positive actuality. In short, they are vortices in the ether—whirling bits of energy—dynamic, never static, pulsating with life, but the life is *spiritual!* As one eminent British scientist put it—"Science now explains matter by *explaining it away!"*

And that, mind you, is what the solid table in front of you is made of, is what your house, your body, the whole world is made of—*whirling bits of energy!*

To quote the *New York Herald-Tribune*: "We used to believe that the universe was composed of an unknown number of different kinds of matter, one kind for each chemical element. The discovery of a new element had all the interest of the unexpected. It might turn out to be anything, to have any imaginable set of properties.

"That romantic prospect no longer exists. We know now that instead of many ultimate kinds of matter there are only two kinds. Both of these are really kinds of electricity. One is negative electricity, being, in fact, the tiny particle called the electron, familiar to radio fans as one of the particles vast swarms of which operate radio vacuum tubes. The other kind of electricity is positive electricity. Its ultimate particles are called protons. From these protons and electrons all of the chemical elements are built up. Iron and lead and oxygen and gold and all the others differ from one another merely in the number and arrangement of the electrons and protons which they contain. That is the modern idea of the nature of matter. *Matter is really nothing but electricity.*

Can you wonder then that scientists believe the time will come when mankind *through mind* can control all this energy, can be absolute master of the winds and the waves? For Modern Science is coming more and more to the belief that what we call *matter is a force subject wholly to the control of mind.*

So it would seem that, to a great degree at least, and perhaps altogether, this world round about us is one of our mind's own creating. And we can put into it, and get from it, pretty much what we wish. "Nothing is..." said Shakespeare, "but thinking makes it so." And the psychologist of today says the same in a different way when he tells us that only those things are real to each individual that he takes into his consciousness. To one with no sense of smell, for instance, there is no such thing as fragrance. To one without a radio, there is no music on the airwaves.

To quote from "*Applied Psychology*," by Warren Hilton:

"The same stimulus acting on different organs of sense will produce different sensations. A blow upon the eye will cause you to see stars; a similar blow upon the ear will cause you to hear an explosive sound. In other words, the vibratory effect of a touch on eye or ear is the same as that of light or sound vibrations.

"The notion you may form of any object in the outer world depends solely upon what part of your brain happens to be connected with that particular nerve-end that received an impression from the object.

"You see the sun without being able to hear it because the only nerve-ends tuned to vibrate in harmony with the ether-waves set in action by the sun are nerve-ends that are connected with the brain center devoted to sight. 'If,' says Professor James, 'we could splice the outer extremities of our optic nerves to our ears, and those of our auditory nerves to our eyes, we should hear the lightning and see the thunder, see the symphony and hear the conductor's movements.'

"In other words, the kind of impressions we receive from the world about us, the sort of mental pictures we form concerning it—in fact, the character of the outer world, the nature of the environment in which our lives are cast—all these things depend for each one of us simply upon how he happens to be put together, upon his individual mental make-up."

In short, it all comes back to the old fable of the three blind men and the elephant. To the one who caught hold of his leg, the elephant was like a tree. To the one who felt of his side, the elephant was like a wall. To the one who seized his tail, the elephant was like a rope. The world is to each one of us the world of his *individual perceptions.*

You are like a radio receiving station. Every moment thousands of impressions are reaching you. You can tune in on whatever ones you like—on joy or sorrow, on success or failure, on optimism or fear. You can select the particular impressions that will best serve you, you can hear only what you want to hear, you can shut out all disagreeable thoughts and sounds and experiences, or you can tune in on discouragement and failure and despair if these are what you want.

Yours is the choice. You have within you a force against which the whole world is powerless. By using it, you can make what you will of life and of your surroundings.

"But," you will say, "objects themselves do not change. It is merely the difference in the way you look at them." Perhaps. But to a great extent, at least, we find what we look for, just as, when we turn the dial on the radio, we tune in on whatever kind of entertainment or instruction we may wish to hear. Who can say that it is not our thoughts that put it there? And why shouldn't it be? All will agree that evil is merely the lack of good, just as darkness is the lack of light. There is infinite good all about us. There is fluid cosmic energy from which to form infinitely more. Why should we not use our thoughts to find the good, or to mold it from the Creative Force all about us? Many scientists believe that we can, and that in proportion as we try to put into our surroundings the good things we desire, rather than the evil ones we fear, *we will find those good things.* Certain it is that we can do this with our own bodies. Just as certain that many people are doing it with the good things of life. They have risen above the conception of life in which matter is the master.

Just as the most powerful forces in nature are the invisible ones—heat, light, air, electricity—so the most powerful forces of man are his invisible forces, his thought forces. And just as electricity can fuse stone and iron, so can your thought forces control your body, so can they win you honor and fortune, so can they make or mar your destiny.

17

From childhood on we are assured on every hand—by scientists, by philosophers, by our religious teachers—that "ours is the earth and the fullness thereof." Beginning with the first chapter of Genesis, we are told that "God said, Let us make man in Our image, after Our likeness; and let them have dominion over the fish of the sea, and over the fowl of the air, and over the cattle, and over all the earth—and over every living thing that moveth upon the earth." All through the Bible, we are repeatedly adjured to use these God-given powers: "The kingdom of God is within you." We hear all this, perhaps we even think we believe, but always, when the time comes to use these God-given talents, there is the "doubt in our heart."

Baudouin expressed it clearly: "To be ambitious for wealth and yet always expecting to be poor; to be always doubting your ability to get what you long for, is like trying to reach east by traveling west. There is no philosophy which will help a man to succeed when he is always doubting his ability to do so, and thus attracting failure. You will go in the direction in which you face...

"There is a saying that every time the sheep bleats, it loses a mouthful of hay. Every time you allow yourself to complain of your lot, to say, 'I am poor; I can never do what others do; I shall never be rich; I have not the ability that others have; I am a failure; luck is against me'; you are laying up so much trouble for yourself.

"No matter how hard you may work for success, If your thought is saturated with the fear of failure, it will kill your efforts, neutralize your endeavors and make success impossible."

What was it made Napoleon the greatest conqueror of his day? Primarily his magnificent faith in Napoleon. He had a sublime belief in his destiny, an absolute confidence that the obstacle was not made which Napoleon could not find a way through, or over, or around. It was only when he lost that confidence, when he hesitated and vacillated for weeks between retreat and advance, that winter caught him in Moscow and ended his dreams of world empire. Fate gave him every chance first. The winter snows were a full month late in coming. But Napoleon hesitated—and was lost. It was not the snows that defeated him. It was not the Russians. It was his loss of faith in himself.

The Kingdom of Heaven

"The Kingdom of Heaven is within you." Heaven is not some faraway state—the reward of years of tribulation here. Heaven is right here—here and now! In the original Greek text, the word used for "Heaven" is "Ouranos." Translated literally, Ouranos means EXPANSION, in other words, a state of being where you can expand, grow, multiply, and increase.

What is the property of a seed? *It spreads*— a single seed will grow into a tree, a single tree will produce enough seeds to plant a great field. And what is the property of leaven or yeast? *It expands*—in a single night it can expand a hundred times in size. So too is the Heaven within us—the power to multiply our happiness, to increase our good, to expand everything we need in life, is within each one of us.

That most of us fail to realize this Heaven—that many are sickly and suffering, that more are ground down by poverty and worry—is no fault of God's. He gave us the power to overcome these evils; the Kingdom of Expansion is within us, the power to increase anything we have. If we fail to find the way to use it, the fault is ours. If we expand the evil instead of the good, that is our misfortune. To enjoy the Heaven that is within us, to begin here and now to live the life eternal, takes only the right understanding and use of the Creative Force working through us.

Even now with the limited knowledge at our command, many people control circumstances to the point of making the world without an expression of their own world within where the real thoughts, the real power, resides. Through this world within, they find the solution of every problem, the cause for every effect. Discover it—and all power, all possession is within your control.

For the world without is but a reflection of that world within. Your thought *creates* the condition your mind images. Keep before your mind's eye the image of all you want to be and you will see it reflected in the world without. Think abundance, feel abundance, BELIEVE abundance, and you will find that as you think and feel and believe, abundance will manifest itself in your daily life. But let fear and worry be your mental companions, thoughts of poverty and limitation dwell in your mind, and worry and fear, limitation and poverty will be your constant companions day and night.

Your mental concept is all that matters. Its relation to matter is that of idea and form. There has got to be an idea before it can take form.

The Creative Force working through you supplies you with limitless energy which will take whatever form your mind demands. Your thoughts are the mold which crystallizes this energy into good or ill according to the form you impress upon it. You are free to choose which. But whichever you choose, the result is sure. Thoughts of wealth, of power, of success, can bring only results commensurate with your idea of them. Thoughts of poverty and lack can bring only limitation and trouble.

"A radical doctrine," you'll say, and think me wildly optimistic. Because the world has been taught for so long to think that some must be rich and some poor, that trials and tribulations are our lot. That this is at best a vale of tears.

The history of the race shows that what is considered to be the learning of one age is ignorance to the next age.

Dr. Edwin E. Slosson, editor of *Science Service,* speaking of the popular tendency to fight against new ideas merely because they are new, said: "All through the history of science, we find that new ideas have to force their way into the common mind in disguise, as though they were burglars instead of benefactors of the race."

And Emerson wrote: "The virtue in most request is conformity. Self-reliance is its aversion. It loves not realities and creators, but names and customs."

In the ages to come, man will look back upon the poverty and wretchedness of so many millions today, and think how foolish we were not to take advantage of the abundant Creative Force all about us. Look at Nature; how profuse she is in everything. Do you suppose the Mind that imaged that profuseness ever intended you to be limited, to have to scrimp and save in order to eke out a bare existence?

There are hundreds of millions of stars in the heavens. Do you suppose the Creative Force which could bring into being worlds without number in such prodigality intended to stint you of the few things necessary to your happiness or well-being?

Nature is prodigal in all that she does. Many insects increase at such a marvelous rate that if it were not for their almost equal death rate, the world would be unable to support them. Rabbits increase so rapidly that a single pair could have 13,000,000 descendants in three years! Fish lay millions of eggs each year. Throughout Nature, everything is lavish. Why should the Creative Force working through you be less generous when it comes to your own supply?

Take as an example the science of numbers. Suppose all numbers were of metal—

that it was against the law to write figures for ourselves. Every time you wanted to do a sum in arithmetic you'd have to provide yourself with a supply of numbers, arrange them in their proper order, work out your problems with them. If your problems were too abstruse you might run out of numbers, have to borrow some from your neighbor or from the bank.

"How ridiculous," you say. "Figures are not things; they are mere ideas, and we can add them or divide them or multiply them as often as we like. Anybody can have all the figures he wants."

To be sure they can. And when you learn to use the Creative Force, you will find that you can multiply your material ideas in the same way. You will EXPAND the good things in your life.

Thought externalizes itself, through the Creative Force working through us. What we are depends entirely upon the images we hold before our mind's eye. Every time we think, we start a chain of causes which will create conditions similar to the thoughts which originated it. Every thought we hold in our consciousness for any length of time becomes impressed upon our subconscious mind and creates a pattern which the Creative Force weaves into our life or environment.

All power is from within and is therefore under our own control. When you can direct your thought processes, you can consciously apply them to any condition, for all that comes to us in the world without is what we've already imaged in the world within. The source of all good, of everything you wish for, is Mind, and you can reach it best through your subconscious. Mind will be to you whatever you believe it to be.

When a man realizes that his mind is part of the God Mind, when he knows that he has only to take any right aspiration to this Universal Mind to see it realized, he loses all sense of worry and fear. He learns to dominate instead of to cringe. He rises to meet every situation, secure in the knowledge that everything necessary to the solution of any problem is in Mind, and that he has but to take his problem to Universal Mind to have it correctly answered.

For if you take a drop of water from the ocean, you know that it has the same properties as all the rest of the water in the ocean, the same percentage of sodium chloride. The only difference between it and the ocean is in volume. If you take a spark of electricity, you know that it has the same properties as the thunderbolt, the same power that moves trains or runs giant machines in factories. Again the only difference is in volume. It is the same with your mind and the God Mind. The only difference between them is in volume. Your mind has the same properties as the God Mind, the same creative genius, the same power over all the earth, the same access to all knowledge. Know this, believe it, use it, and "yours is the earth and the fullness thereof." In the exact proportion that you believe yourself to be part of the God Mind, sharing in Its all-power, in that proportion can you demonstrate the mastery over your own body and over the world about you.

All growth, all supply is from the Creative Force working through you. If you would have power, if you would have wealth, you must first form the mold in this world within, in your subconscious mind, through belief and understanding.

If you would remove discord, you must remove the wrong images—images of ill health, of worry and trouble from within. The trouble with most of us is that we live entirely in the world without. We have no knowledge of that inner world which is responsible for all the conditions we meet and all the experiences we have. We have no conception of "the Father that is within us."

The inner world promises us life and health, prosperity and happiness—dominion over all the earth, it promises peace and perfection for all its offspring. It gives you the right way and the adequate way to accomplish any normal purpose. Business, labor, professions, exist primarily in thought. And the outcome of your labors in them is regulated by thought. Consider the difference, then, in this outcome if you have at your command only the limited capacity of your conscious mind, compared with the boundless energy of the subconscious and of the Creative Force working through it. "Thought, not money, is the real business capital," says Harvey S. Firestone, "and if you know absolutely that what you are doing is right, then you are bound to accomplish it in due season."

Thought is a dynamic energy with the power to bring its object out from the Creative Force all about us. Matter is unintelligent. Thought can shape and control. Every form in which matter is today is but the expression of some thought, some desire, some idea.

You have a mind. You can originate thought. And thoughts are creative. Therefore you can create for yourself that which you desire. Once you realize this, you are taking a long step toward success in whatever undertaking you have in mind. You are the potter. You are continually forming images—good or bad. Why not consciously form only good images?

More than half the prophecies in the scriptures refer to the time when man shall possess the earth, when tears and sorrow shall be unknown, and peace and plenty shall be everywhere. That time will come. It is nearer than most people think possible. You are helping it along. Every man or woman who is honestly trying to use the power of mind in the right way is doing their part in the great cause. For it is only through Mind that peace and plenty can be gained. The earth is laden with

22

treasures as yet undiscovered. But they are every one of them known to the God Mind, for it was this Mind that first imaged them there. And, as part of Universal Mind, they can be known to you.

"To the Manner Born"

Few of us have any idea of our mental powers. The old idea was that man must take this world as he found it. He'd been born into a certain position in life, and to try to rise above his fellows was not only the height of bad taste, but sacrilegious as well. An All-wise Providence had decreed by birth the position a child should occupy in the web of organized society. For him to be discontented with his lot, for him to attempt to raise himself to a higher level, was tantamount to tempting Providence. The gates of Hell yawned wide for such scatterbrains, who were lucky if in this life they incurred nothing worse than the ribald scorn of their associates.

That is the system that produced aristocracy and feudalism. That is the system that feudalism and aristocracy strove to perpetuate. But the basis of all democracies is that man is not bound by any system, that he need not accept the world as he finds it. He can remake the world to his own ideas. It is merely the raw material. He can make what he will of it.

It is this idea that is responsible for all our inventions, all our progress. Man is satisfied with nothing. He is constantly remaking his world. And now more than ever will this be true, for psychology teaches us that each one has within themselves the power to use the Creative Force to become what they will.

LEARN TO CONTROL YOUR THOUGHT. Learn to image upon your mind only the things you want to see reflected there.

You will never improve yourself by dwelling upon the drawbacks of your neighbors. You will never attain perfect health and strength by thinking of weakness or disease. No man ever made a perfect score by watching his rival's target. You have to think strength, think health, think riches. To paraphrase Pascal—"Our achievements today are but the sum of our thoughts of yesterday."

For yesterday is the mold in which the Creative Force flowing through us took shape. And cosmic energy concentrated for any definite purpose becomes power. To those who perceive the nature and transcendency of this Force, all physical power sinks into insignificance.

What is imagination but a form of thought? Yet it is the instrument by which all the inventors and discoverers have opened the way to new worlds. Those who grasp this force, be their state ever so humble, their natural gifts ever so insignificant, become our leading men and women. They are our governors and supreme lawgivers, the guides of the drifting host that follows them as by an irrevocable decree. To quote Glenn Clark in the *Atlantic Monthly,* "Whatever we have of civilization is their work, theirs alone. If progress was made, they made it. If spiritual facts were discerned, they discerned them. If justice and order were put in place of insolence and chaos, they wrought the change. Never is progress achieved by the masses. Creation ever remains the task of the individual."

Our railroads, our telephones, our automobiles, our libraries, our newspapers, our thousands of other conveniences, comforts and necessities are due to the creative genius of but two percent of our population. And the same two percent own a great percentage of the wealth of the country.

The question arises, Who are they? What are they? The sons of the rich? College men? No—few of them had any early advantages. Many of them have never seen the inside of a college. It was grim necessity that drove them, and somehow, some way, they found a method of drawing upon their Creative Force, and through that Force they reached success.

You don't need to stumble and grope. You can call upon the Creative Force at will. There are three steps necessary:

First, to realize that you have the power. Second, to know what you want. Third, to center your thought upon it with singleness of purpose. To accomplish these steps takes only a fuller understanding of the Power-that-is-within-you.

So let us make use of this dynamo, which is *you*. What is going to start it working? Your *Faith,* the faith that is begotten of understanding. Faith is the impulsion of this power within. Faith is the confidence, the assurance, the enforcing truth, the knowing that the right idea of life will bring you into the reality of existence and the manifestation of the All power.

All cause is in Mind—and Mind is everywhere. All the knowledge there is, all the power there is, is all about you—no matter where you may be. Your mind is part of it. You have access to it. If you fail to avail yourself of it, you have no one to blame but yourself. For as the drop of water in the ocean shares in all the properties of the rest of the ocean water, so you share in that all-power, all-wisdom of Mind. If you have been sick and ailing, if poverty and hardship have been your lot, don't blame it on "fate." Blame yourself.

"Yours is the earth and everything that's in it." But you've got to take it. The Creative Force is there—but you must use it. It is round about you like the air you breathe. You don't expect others to do your breathing for you. Neither can you expect them to use the Creative Force for you. Universal Intelligence is not only the mind of the Creator of the universe, but it is also the mind of MAN, your intelligence, your mind.

I am success, though hungry, cold, ill-clad, I wander for awhile, I smile and say, "It is but a time, I shall be glad Tomorrow, for good fortune comes my way. God is my Father, He has wealth untold, His wealth is mine, health, happiness and gold."

—ELLA WHEELER WILCOX

So start today by knowing that you can do anything you wish to do, have anything you wish to have, be anything you wish to be. The rest will follow.

A Funny World

*There is a world, a funny world, that's not a world at all;
A world that has no shape nor size, that's neither sphere nor ball;
You think at first that it exists; you think it very true;
Then, finally, you see the point: that it's just fooling you.*

*Perhaps, you once lived in this world with all its hates and fears;
You were a glum and saddened soul, believed in pains and tears;
You thought you had to be diseased and thought there was a hell;
When, all at once, you learned the truth. This world just went pell-mell.*

*And, then, this world, this shadow world, just disappeared from sight;
And in its place a world of joy, of health, of love and light
Came into view right where you were; you came to understand
That you abide in Heaven now and God is right at hand.*

—FRANK BLENLARRY WHITNEY

The Goal

If you think you can win, your battle is won! Whatever you need you can have, you'll find: It's all in the way you set your mind.

If you feel that your part in the world is small, You may never achieve your work at all; But feel that your life, of God's life is a part—Then you'll work in the way you have set your heart.

If you know you are great, you will do great things; Your thoughts will soar on eagle's wings; Your life will reach its destined goal, If you know the way to set your soul.

— KATHERINE W ILDER RUGGLES

CHAPTER 2

THE URGE

WHAT IS THE STRONGEST force in life? What is the power that carries those who heed it from the bottommost pits of poverty to the top of the world—from the slums and ghettos to governorships and presidencies and the rulership of kingdoms?

The URGE for SECURITY—for ASSURED SUBSISTENCE AND SAFETY!

When the first primitive water plants appeared, living in the saturated soil along the shores of the waters, you might think the Creative Force would have rested content for a while. It had created something that lived and grew and reproduced itself. It was the first form of life upon this earth— the thallophytes.

As with the water plants, there came next the multiple-celled creature, each dependent for life upon drawing its own nourishment from the waters about. Then a central system corresponding with the stem and roots of the fern, finally evolving into distinct organs to take care of each function of life. And so was laid the foundation for all forms of animal life that have developed from this simple beginning. The principle had been perfected—it remained now only to develop every possible ramification of it, until the highest form should be reached.

When means of protection were found necessary for survival, the Creative Force developed these too. For those subject to the abrasive effects of sand and rocks, it developed shells. To the weak, it gave means of escape. To the strong, teeth and claws with which to fight. It fitted each form to meet the conditions it had to cope with. When size was the paramount consideration, it made the Gigantosaurus, over a hundred feet long and as big as a house and all the other giant monsters of antiquity. When smallness was the objective, it developed the tiny insects and water creatures, so that it takes a powerful microscope to see them, yet so perfectly made as to form organisms as exact and well-regulated as the greatest.

Size, strength, fierceness, speed—all these it developed to the last degree. It tried every form of life, but each had its weaknesses, each was vulnerable in some way.

The Creative Force might develop forms that would grow, but nothing physical could be made that would be invulnerable, that would ever attain SECURITY.

To man has been given the job of emulating his Maker — of becoming a creator, finding new and broader and better ways through which to express the Creative Force in him. His is the work of creating beauty, or bringing more of comfort, of joy and happiness into the world.

To every living thing on earth is given a measure of Creative Power. Of the lower forms of life all that is required is that they bring forth fruit according to their kind—"some thirty, some sixty, some an hundred fold."

Of you, however, much more is expected. To bring forth fruit according to your physical kind is good—but that is no more than the animals do. More is required of you. You must bring forth fruit, according to your mental kind as well! You are a son of God, a creator. Therefore creation is expected of you. You are to spread seeds not merely of human kind, but of the intellect as well.

You are to leave the world a better place than you found it, with more of joy in it, more of beauty, of comfort, of understanding, of light.

The real purpose of Life is expression, the constant urge onward and upward. Even in the smallest child, you see evidence of this. It plays with blocks. Why? To express the urge in him to build something. The growing boy makes toys, builds a hut. The girl sews dresses, cares for dolls, cooks, plays house. Why? To give vent to the inner urge in each, struggling for expression.

They reach the period of adolescence. They dance, they motor, they seek all manner of thrill. Why? Again to satisfy that constant craving of the Creative Force in them for *expression!*

True—at the moment, it is mostly a physical urge. But in some way, that urge must be translated into a mental one—*and satisfied!* It must be given an outlet for expression. It must be brought into the light of day, given useful, uplifting work to do, and it will then bring forth abundant fruit of happiness and accomplishment. Because no matter how it is repressed, no matter how deep it is buried in dark cellars, the Creative Force will still bring forth fruit—only then it may be fungus growths of sin and misery.

Through every man there flows this Creative Force, with infinite power to draw to itself whatever is necessary to its expression. It doesn't matter who you are, what your environment or education or advantages, the Creative Force in you has the same power for good or evil. Mind you, that Force never brings forth evil. Its life is good. But just as you can graft onto the trunk of the finest fruit tree a branch of the upas tree, and thereupon bring forth deadly fruit, so can you engraft upon the pure energy of your Creative Force any manner of fruit you desire. But if the fruit be bad, it is you who are to blame, not the perfect Force that flows through you.

"To every man there openeth

A high way and a low,

And every man decideth

The way his soul shall go."

What is it makes a poor immigrant boy like Edward Bok overcome every handicap of language and education, to become one of the greatest editors the country has ever known?

Isn't it that the more circumstances conspire to repress it, the stronger becomes the urge of the Creative Force in you for expression? The more it lacks channels through which to expand, the more inclined it is to burst its shell and flow forth in all directions.

It is the old case of the river that is dammed generating the most power. Most of us are so placed that some opportunity for expression is made easy for us. And that little opportunity serves like a safety valve to a boiler—it leaves us steam enough to do something worthwhile, yet keeps us from getting up enough power to burst the shell about us, and sweep away every barrier that holds us down.

Yet it is only such an irresistible head of steam as that which makes great successes. That is why the blow which knocks all the props from under us is often the turning point in our whole career.

You cannot stand still. You must go forward—or see the world slide past you. This was well illustrated by figures worked out by Russell Conwell years ago. Of all the thousands who are left fortunes through the deaths of relatives, *only one in seventeen dies wealthy!*

Why? Because the fortunes left them take away the need for initiative on their part. Their money gives to them easy means of expressing the urge in them, without effort on their part. It gives them dozens of safety valves, through which their steam continually escapes.

The result is that they not only accomplish nothing worthwhile, but they soon dissipate the fortunes that were left them. They are like kettles, the urge of life keeping the water at boiling point, but the open spout of ease letting the steam escape as fast as it forms, until presently there is not even any water left.

Why do the sons of rich men so seldom accomplish anything worthwhile? Because they don't have to. Every opportunity is given them to turn the Creative Force in them through pleasant channels, and they dissipate through these the energies that might carry them to any height. The result? They never have a strong enough "head of steam" left to carry through any real job.

You are a channel for power. There is no limit to the amount of Creative Force that will flow through you. The only limit to what you *get,* is the amount that you *use.* Like the widow's cruse, no matter how much you pour out, there is just as much still available, but unlike the cruse of oil, your channel and your power grow with use!

What are *you* doing to satisfy the urge in you? What are you doing to give expression—*and increase*—to the Creative Force working through you?

Many a man and woman has the urge to write—or paint—or sing—or do some other worthwhile thing. But does he? No, indeed. He is not well enough known, or has not the right training, or lacks education or opportunity or influence. Or else she has tried once or twice and failed.

What does that matter? It is not your responsibility if others fail in their appreciation. Your job is to express the Creative Force surging through you, to give it the best you have. Each time you do that, you are the better for it, whether others care for it or not. And each time you will give more perfect, more understanding expression to the Creative Force working through you, until sooner or later ALL appreciate it.

You don't suppose the great writers, the successful artists, were born with the ability to write or paint, do you? You don't suppose they had all the latest books or finest courses on the art of expression? On the contrary, all that many of them had was the URGE! The rest they had to acquire just as you do.

The Creative Force flowing through you is as perfect as the rose in the bud. But just as the life in the rose bush evolved through millions of less beautiful forms before it perfected the rose, so must you be satisfied to model but crudely at first, in the sure knowledge that if you keep giving of your best, eventually the product of your hands or your brain will be as perfect as the rose.

Every desire, every urge of your being, is Creative Force straining at the bonds of repression you have put upon it, straining for expression. You can't stand still. You can't stop and smugly say—"Look what I did yesterday, or last week, or last year!" It is what you are doing now that counts.

The Creative Force is dynamic. It is ever seeking expression—and when you fail to provide new and greater outlets for it, it slips away to work through some more ambitious soul who will. Genius is nothing but the irresistible urge for one particular channel of expression—an urge so strong that it is like a mountain torrent in flood, sweeping trees and bridges and dams and everything else before it.

So don't worry about whether those around you recognize your talents. Don't mind if the world seems indifferent to them. The world is too busy with its own little ways of expressing life to pay much attention to yours. To get under its skin, you must do something to appeal to its emotions.

You see, the world in the mass is like a child. Prod it, and you make it angry. Preach to it, or try to teach or uplift it, and you lose its attention. You bore it. But appeal to its emotions—make it laugh or weep—and it will love you! Love you and lavish upon you all the gifts in its power to give. That is why it pays a Crosby millions, and a great educator only hundreds. Yet the name of the educator may live for ages, while the entertainer will be remembered only until a better one displaces him.

So forget the immediate rewards the world has to offer, and give your energies to finding ways of better expressing the Creative Force in you. You are expressing it every day and hour. Try to express it better, to find ever-greater channels through which to work. If your urge is to write a story, put into it the best you have, no matter if you know you could get by with a third of the effort. Work always for perfection, knowing that thus only can you be sure of the greatest help of the Creative Force working through you.

That Creative Force is striving for a perfect body, perfect surroundings, perfect work. It is not its fault when you manifest less than these. Depend upon it, it is not satisfied with anything less. So don't you be! If you have the courage to refuse anything short of your ideal, if you have the dogged perseverance to keep trying, there's no power in the heavens or the earth that can keep you from success!

It's the way every great success has been won. Do you suppose if a Michelangelo or Da Vinci had an off day and painted some imperfect figures into a painting, he left them there? Do you think he explained to his friends that he was under the weather that day, and so, while he was sorry it spoiled the picture, he could not be

31

held accountable for it?

Just imagine one of these great painters letting something less than his best go over his name! Why, he would cheerfully destroy a year's work rather than have that happen. The moment he noticed it, he would hasten to scratch out the offensive figure, lest others might see it and judge his work by it. Or even if no one was ever to see it, he would do it because it failed to express the genius that was his!

That is how you must feel about your work before ever it can attain greatness. The Creative Force working through you is perfect, all-powerful, without limit. So don't ever be satisfied with less than its best! Follow its urge. Use every atom of strength and skill and riches you have to express it, serene in the knowledge that you can do anything through the God working in you.

Andrew Carnegie said:

"Here is the prime condition of success, the great secret: Concentrate your energy, thought, and capital exclusively upon the business in which you are engaged. Having begun on one line, resolve to fight it out on that line, to lead in it, adopt every improvement, have the best machinery, and know the most about it. Finally, do not be impatient, for, as Emerson says, 'No one can cheat you out of ultimate success but yourself.' "

Have you ever climbed a high mountain? Did you notice, as you kept getting higher and higher, how your horizon rose with you? It is the same with life. The more you use the Creative Force, the more you have to use. Your skill and power and resources grow with your use of them.

From earliest infancy, the Creative Force is trying to express something through you. First it is purely physical—a perfect body, and through it the generation of other perfect bodies. But gradually it rises above the physical plane, and strives to express itself in some way that will leave the world a better place for your having been in it—a memory of noble thoughts, of splendid deeds, of obstacles conquered and ideals won.

Do your part by never falling short of your best, no matter in how small a thing you may express it. Perfection, you remember, is made up of trifles, but perfection is no trifle.

It doesn't matter how small or seemingly unimportant your job may be. You have the same chance to attain perfection in it as the greatest artist has in his work. It

32

doesn't matter how little others may believe that any good or great thing can come from you. Who knows what good things may come from you?

"There's nothing to fear—you're as good as the best, As strong as the mightiest, too. You can win in every battle or test; For there's no one just like you. There's only one you in the world today; So nobody else, you see, Can do your work in as fine a way,

"You're the only you there'll be! So face the world, and all life is yours To conquer and love and live; And you'll find the happiness that endures In just the measure you give:

There's nothing too good for you to possess,
Nor heights where you cannot go;
Your power is more than belief or guess—
It's something you have to know.
There's nothing to fear—you can and you will,
For you're the invincible you.
So set your foot on the highest hill—
There's nothing you cannot do."

—ANONYMOUS

CHAPTER 3

THE MENTAL EQUIVALENT

"All the world's a stage, And all the men and women merely players."

WHAT PART ARE YOU acting in the theater of life? What place have you assigned to yourself on that stage? Are you one of the stars? Do you bear one of the important parts? Or are you merely one of the "mob" scene, just background for the action, or one of the "props" for moving the scenery around?

Whatever part is yours, it is you who have given it to you, for as Emerson says, and the whole Bible teaches from one end to the other, "Man surrounds himself with the true image of himself."

"Every spirit builds itself a house," writes Emerson, "and beyond its house a world, and beyond its world a heaven. Know then that the world exists for you. For you is the phenomenon perfect. What we are, that only can we see. All that Adam had, all that Caesar could, you have and can do. Adam called his house, heaven and earth, Caesar called his house, Rome; you perhaps call yours a cobbler's trade; a hundred acres of plowed land; or a scholar's garret. Yet line for line and point for point, your dominion is as great as theirs, though without fine names. Build therefore your own world. As fast as you conform your life to the pure idea in your mind, that will unfold its great proportions."

All men are created free and equal, in that all are given the only tool with which you can really build your life. That tool is your thought. All have the same material with which to build. That material is the Creative Force working through you. As your interior thought is, so will your exterior life be. The Creative Force takes shape in the mold your thoughts give it. "We think in secret and it comes to pass; environment is but our looking glass."

"In all my lectures," declared Emerson, "I have taught one doctrine—the infinitude of the private man, the ever-availability to every man of the divine presence within his own mind, from which presence he draws, at his need, inexhaustible power."

"Think big, and your deeds will grow; Think small, and you'll fall behind;

Think that you can, and you will— It's all in the state of mind."

"What sort of mental image do you hold of yourself?" Emmet Fox asks in one of his helpful books. "Whatever your real conviction of yourself is, that is what you will demonstrate.

"Whatever enters into your life is but the material expression of some belief of your own mind. The kind of body you have, the kind of home you have, the kind of job you have, the kind of people you meet with, are all conditioned by and correspond to the mental concept you are holding. The Bible teaches that from beginning to end.

"About twenty years ago, I coined the phrase 'mental equivalent.' And I am going to say that anything that you want in your life, anything that you would like to have in your life—a healthy body, a satisfactory vocation, friends, opportunities, above all the understanding of God—if you want these things to come into your life, you must furnish a mental equivalent for them. Supply yourself with a mental equivalent and the thing must come to you. Without a mental equivalent, it cannot come to you."

And what is this "Mental Equivalent"? What but your mental image of what you hope to be, plan to be. "Think and forms spring into shape, will and worlds disintegrate."

God hid the whole world in your heart, as one great writer tells us, so when any object or purpose is clearly held in thought, its manifestation in tangible and visible form is merely a question of time. Cause and effect are as absolute and undeviating in the hidden realm of thought as in the world of visible and material things. Mind is the master weaver, both of the interior garment of character and the outer garment of circumstance. Thinking for a purpose brings that purpose into being just as surely as a hen's "setting" on an egg matures and brings the chicken into being.

"Amid all the mysteries by which we are surrounded," wrote Herbert Spencer, "nothing is more certain than that we are ever in the presence of an infinite and eternal energy from which all things proceed."

That Infinite and eternal energy or Creative Force is molded by our thought. For thousands of years, men of wisdom have realized this and have molded their own lives accordingly. The Prophets of old did their best to impress this fact upon their people. "My word (my thought or mental image) shall not come back to me void, but shall accomplish that whereunto it was sent," says one. And in a hundred places, you will find the same thought expressed. You are molding your tomorrows, whether you realize it or not. Make them the good you desire—not the evil you fear.

Clarence Edwin Flynn expresses something of the power of thought in his little poem:

"Whenever you cultivate a thought Remember it will trace With certain touch, its pictured form A story on your face.

"Whenever you dwell upon a thought, Remember it will roll Into your being and become A fiber of your soul.

"Whenever you send out a thought, Remember it will be A force throughout the universe, For all eternity."

Remember that this holds good in all of your affairs. In your own thoughts, you are continually dramatizing yourself, your environment, your circumstances. If you see yourself as prosperous, you will be. If you see yourself as continually hard up, that is exactly what you will be. If you are constantly looking for slights, if you seek trouble in your thoughts, you will not be long in finding them in your daily life. Whatever part you give yourself in the drama of life in your own thought, that part you will eventually act out on the stage of life.

So give yourself a good part. Make yourself the hero of the piece, rather than the downtrodden member of the mob or the overworked servant. Set your lines in pleasant places. It is just as easy as laying them in the slums. As long as you are bound to dramatize yourself and your surroundings and circumstances anyway, try this:

1 Dramatize yourself, in your mind's eye, with the people and surroundings and things you want most, doing the things you would like most to do, holding the sort of position you long for, doing the work you feel yourself best fitted to do. Some may call it daydreaming, but make it daydreaming with a purpose. Make the picture as clear in your mind's eye as though you saw it on the screen of a motion picture theater. And get all the enjoyment out of it that you can. Believe in it. Be thankful for it.

2Prove your faith in your dream by making every logical preparation for the material manifestation of your desires. Just as the kings of old did when they prayed for water, dig your ditches to receive it.

3Alter minor details of your drama as you like, but stick to the main goal. Make it your objective, and like Grant in his successful campaign, resolve to stick to it "though it takes all summer."

4Be a finisher as well as a beginner. Remember that one job finished is worth a dozen half finished. The three-quarter horses never win a prize. It is only at the finish that the purse awaits you. So complete your drama mentally before you begin to act it out, and then stick to it actually until you've made it manifest for all to see.

5Keep that mental drama to yourself. Don't tell it to others. Remember Samson. He could do anything as long as he kept his mouth shut. Most people's minds are like boilers with the safety valve wide open. They never get up enough of a head of steam to run their engines. Keep your plans to yourself. That way they'll generate such power that you won't need to tell others about them —they'll see the result for themselves.

"The imagination," says Glenn Clark in "The Soul's Sincere Desire," "is of all qualities in man the most Godlike—that which associates him most closely with God. The first mention we read of man in the Bible is where he is spoken of as an 'image.' 'Let us make man in our image, after our likeness.' The only place where an image can be conceived is in the Imagination. Thus man, the highest creation of God, was a creation of God's imagination.

"The source and center of all man's creative power—the power that above all others lifts him above the level of brute creation, and that gives him dominion, is his power of making images, or the power of the imagination. There are some who have always thought that the imagination was something which makes-believe that which is not. This is fancy—not imagination. Fancy would convert that which is real into pretense and sham; imagination enables one to see through the appearance of a thing to what it really is."

There is a very real law of cause and effect which makes the dream of the dreamer come true. It is the law of visualization—the law that calls into being in this outer material world everything that is real in the inner world by directing your Creative Force into it. Imagination pictures the thing you desire. VISION idealizes it. It reaches beyond the thing that is, into the conception of what can be. Imagination gives you the picture. Vision gives you the impulse to make the picture your own by directing your Creative Force into it.

Make your mental image clear enough, picture it vividly in every detail, then do everything you can to bring that image into being, and the Creative Force working through you will speedily provide whatever is necessary to make it an everyday reality.

The law holds true of everything in life. There is nothing you can rightfully desire that cannot be brought into being through visualization and faith.

The keynote of successful visualization is this: See things as you would have them be instead of as they are. Close your eyes and make clear mental pictures. Make them look and act just as they would in real life. In short, daydream—but daydream purposefully. Concentrate on the one idea to the exclusion of all others, and continue to concentrate on that one idea until it has been accomplished.

Do you want an automobile? A home? A factory? They can all be won in the same way. They are in their essence all of them ideas of mind, and if you will but build them up in your own mind first, complete in every detail, you will find that the Creative Force working through you can build them up similarly in the material world.

"The building of a trans-continental railroad from a mental picture," says C. W. Chamberlain in *The Uncommon Sense of Applied Psychology*," "gives the average individual an idea that it is a big job. The fact of the matter is, the achievement, as well as the perfect mental picture, is made up of millions of little jobs, each fitting in its proper place and helping to make up the whole. A skyscraper is built from individual bricks, the laying of each brick being a single job which must be completed before the next brick can be laid."

It is the same with any work, any study. To quote Professor James:

"As we become permanent drunkards by so many separate drinks, so we become saints in the moral, and authorities and experts in the practical and scientific spheres, by so many separate acts and hours of working. Let no youth have any anxiety about the upshot of his education whatever the line of it may be. If he keep faithfully busy each hour of the working day he may safely leave the final result to itself. He can with perfect certainty count on waking some fine morning, to find himself one of the competent ones of his generation, in whatever pursuit he may have singled out...Young people should know this truth in advance. The ignorance of it has probably engendered more discouragement and faintheartedness in youths embarking on arduous careers than all other causes taken together."

Remember that the only limit to your capabilities is the one you place upon them. There is no law of limitation. The only law is of supply. Through mind you can draw upon the Creative Force for anything you wish. Use it! There are no limitations upon it. Don't put any on yourself.

Aim high! If you miss the moon, you may hit a star. Everyone admits that this world and all the vast firmament must have been thought into shape from the formless void by some God-Mind. That same God-Mind rules today, and it has given to each form of life power to attract to itself as much of the Creative Force as it needs for its perfect growth. The tree, the plant, the animal—each one finds supply to meet its need.

You are an intelligent, reasoning creature. Your mind is part of the great God-Mind. And you have the power to *say* what you require for perfect growth. Don't sell yourself short; don't sell yourself for a penny. Whatever price you set upon yourself, life will give. So aim high. Demand much! Make a clear, distinct mental image of what it is you want. Hold it in your thoughts. Visualize it, see it, *believe it!* The ways and means of satisfying that desire will follow. For supply always comes on the heels of demand.

It is by doing this that you take your fate out of the hands of chance. It is in this way that you control the experiences you are to have in life. But be sure to visualize *only what you want.* The law works both ways. If you visualize your worries and your fears, you will make them real. Control your thought and you control circumstances. Conditions will be what you make them.

To paraphrase Thackeray—"The world is a looking glass, and gives back to every man the reflection of his own thought."

Philip of Macedon, Alexander's father, perfected the "phalanx"—a triangular formation which enabled him to center the whole weight of his attack on one point in the opposing line. It drove through everything opposed to it. In that day and age it was invincible. And the idea is just as invincible today.

Keep the one thought in mind, SEE it being carried out step by step, and you can knit any group of workers into one homogeneous whole, all centered on the one idea. You can accomplish any one thing. You can put across any definite idea. Keep that mental picture ever in mind and you will make it as invincible as was Alexander's phalanx of old.

"It is not the guns or armament
Or the money they can pay,
It's the close cooperation
That makes them win the day.
It is not the individual

Or the army as a whole
But the everlasting team work
Of every bloomin' soul."

—J.MASON KNOX

The error of the ages is the tendency mankind has always shown to limit the power of Mind, or its willingness to help in time of need. We may know that we are "temples of the Living God." We may even be proud of that fact. But we never take advantage of it to dwell in that temple, to proclaim dominion over things and conditions. We never avail ourselves of the power that is ours.

The great prophets of old had the forward look. Theirs was the era of hope and expectation. They looked for the time when the revelation should come that was to make men "sons of God." "They shall obtain joy and gladness, and sorrow and sighing shall flee away."

The world has turned in vain to materialistic philosophy for deliverance from its woes. In the future the only march of actual progress will be in the mental realm, and this progress will not be in the way of human speculation and theorizing, but in the actual demonstration of the power of Mind to mold the Creative Force into anything of good. The world stands today within the vestibule of the vast realm of divine Intelligence, wherein is found the transcendent, practical power of Mind over all things.

CHAPTER 4

I AM

YEARS AGO, Emlie Coué electrified the world with his cures of all manner of disease—solely through the power of SUGGESTION!

"Nobody ought to be sick!" he proclaimed, and proceeded to prove it by curing hundreds who came to him after doctors had failed to relieve them. Not only that, but he showed that the same methods could be used to cure one's affairs—to bring riches instead of debts, success instead of drudgery.

Originally, Coué was a hypnotist. In his little drug store, he found occasional patients whom he could hypnotize. He hypnotized them—put their conscious minds to sleep—and addressed himself directly to their subconscious.

To the subconscious, he declared that there was nothing wrong with whatever organ the patient had thought diseased, and the subconscious accepted the statement and molded the Creative Force within accordingly. When the patient came out from under the hypnotic influence, he was well! It remained then only to convince his conscious mind of this, so he would not send through new suggestions of disease to his subconscious, and the patient was cured!

How account for that? By the fact that the disease or imperfection is not so much in your body as in your mind. It is in your rate of motion, and this is entirely mind-controlled. Change the subconscious belief, and the physical manifestations change with it. You speed up your rate of motion, and in that way throw off the discordant elements of disease. Doctors recognize this when they give their patients harmless sugar pills, knowing that these will dispel fear, and that when the images conjured up by fear are gone, the supposed trouble will go with them.

But Coué found many patients whom he could not hypnotize. How treat them? By inducing a sort of self-hypnosis in themselves. It is a well-known fact that constant repetition carries conviction—especially to the subconscious mind. So Coué had his patients continually repeat to themselves the affirmation that their trouble was passing, that they were getting better and better. "Every day in every way I am getting better and better." And this unreasoning affirmation cured thousands of ills that had been troubling them for years.

What is back of that success? A law as old as the hills, a law that has been known to psychologists for years—the law that the subconscious mind accepts as true anything that is repeated to it convincingly and often. And once it has accepted such a statement as true, it proceeds to mold the Creative Force working through it in such wise as to MAKE IT TRUE!

You see, where the conscious mind reasons inductively, the subconscious uses only deductive reasoning. Where the reasoning mind weighs each fact that is presented to it, questions the truth or falsity of each, and then forms its conclusions accordingly, the subconscious acts quite differently. IT ACCEPTS AS FACT ANY STATEMENT THAT IS PRESENTED TO IT CONVINCINGLY. Then, having accepted this as the basis of its actions, it proceeds logically to do all in its power to bring it into being.

That is why the two most important words in the English language are the words —"I AM." That is why the Ancients regarded these two words as the secret name of God.

You ask a friend how he is, and he replies carelessly—"I am sick, I am poor, I am unlucky, I am subject to this, that or the other thing,"—never stopping to think that by those very words he is fastening misfortune upon himself, declaring to the subconscious mind within him that he IS sick or poor or weak or the servant of some desire.

"Let the weak say—'I am strong!'" the Prophet Joel exhorted his people thousands of years ago. And the advice is as good today as it was then.

You have seen men, under hypnotic suggestion, perform prodigies of strength. You have seen them with their bodies stretched between two chairs, their heads on one, their feet on another, supporting the weight of several people standing on them, when they could not ordinarily hold up even their own bodies in that position. How can they do it? Because the hypnotist has assured their subconscious that they CAN do it, that they have the strength and power necessary.

"Therefore I say unto you, what things so ever ye desire when ye pray, BELIEVE THAT YE RECEIVE THEM, and ye shall HAVE them." How can you work up the necessary faith to accomplish the things you desire? By taking the advice of the wise men of old, of the Prophet Joel—by claiming it as yours, and setting your subconscious mind to work making those claims come true.

It is a sort of self-hypnosis, but so is all of prayer. Away back in 1915, the head of the Warsaw Psychological Institute conducted a series of experiments from which he concluded that the energy manifested by anyone during life is in direct ratio with his power for plunging himself into a condition of auto-hypnosis. In simple language, that means convincing yourself of the possibility of doing the things you want to do.

The subconscious in each of us HAS the knowledge, HAS the power to do any right thing we may require of it. The only need is to implant in it the confidence— the "BELIEVE THAT YOU RECEIVE".

In a case cited by Baudouin, the famous psychologist, a woman after using auto-suggestion as a means of helping herself, declared: "I can do twice as much work as before. During vacation, I have been able to go through two extensive tasks, such as a year ago I should never have attempted. This year I systematized my work and said, 'I can do it all; what I am undertaking is materially possible, and therefore must be morally possible; consequently I ought not to experience, and shall not experience, discouragement, hesitancy, annoyance, or slackness.' " As a result of these affirmations, the way to her inner powers was opened and she was able to say truly, "Nothing could stop me, nothing could prevent my doing what I had planned to do; you might almost have said that things were done by themselves, without the slightest effort on my part." Not only did she find herself working with a high degree of success heretofore unknown, but with a certainty and calmness of mind beyond her previous attainment.

Emerson, with his genius for condensing great truths into a few words, wrote —"Do the thing and you shall have the power."

The wise men of old learned thousands of years ago that life is like an echo. It always returns the call sent out. Like the echo, the response is always the same as the call, and the louder the call, the greater the response.

You say—"I am sick, I am poor," and your words are forerunners of your circumstance. "Every idle word that men shall speak, they shall give account of in the day of judgment." And that day of judgment comes sooner than most people think.

Be careful to speak only those words which you are willing to see take form in your life, for remember the words of wise old Job: "Thou shalt also decree a thing, and it shall be established unto thee." Never speak the word of lack or limitation, for—"By thy words shall thou be justified, and by thy words shalt thou be condemned."

Affirm constantly—"I have faith in the power of my word. I speak only that which I desire to see made manifest." Remember, "Behind you is Infinite Power, before you is endless possibility, around you is endless opportunity. Why should you fear?"

C. G. Tanner expresses the idea beautifully—

"If you have faith in what you want to do,
If you behold yourself a king's own son,
Then you have asked God's power to work through you,
And pledged yourself to see that it is done.
'With faith I place it in God's hands,' you say?
God's hands are yours! Your good must come through you!
God has no other hands with which He may
Give unto you your sonship's rightful due.

"Faith and persistence travel hand in hand,
The one without the other incomplete.
If you would reach success, then take the stand,
'This I will try once more,' and no defeat
Can cloud that beacon gleaming bright and clear,
Or conjure up dread failure's haunting wraith!
You rest secure with God. No thought of fear
Can dim the shining armor of your faith."

Most people seem to think that we work to live, but there is a deeper purpose in life than that. What we really work for is to call forth the talents that are within our own soul, to give expression to the Creative Force working through us. That is the one big purpose for which we were born—to express the Creative Force in us, to give God the chance to express Himself through us. And we CAN do it. As the famous English poet Shelley put it—"The Almighty has given men arms long enough to reach the stars, if they would but put them forth."

And the first step lies in using what you have. The key to power lies in using, not hoarding. Use releases still more power for ever-greater works. Hoarding builds a hard shell around the thing hoarded and prevents more from coming in. You may have what you want, if you are willing to use what you have now. You can do what you want to do if you are willing to do what there is to do right now. "The one condition coupled with the gift of truth," says Emerson, *"is its use."*

Professor William Bateson of the British Society for Scientific Research said: "We are finding now beyond doubt that the gifts and geniuses of mankind are due not so much to something added to the ordinary person, but instead are due to factors which in the normal person INHIBIT the development of these gifts. They are now without doubt to be looked upon as RELEASES of powers normally suppressed."

And why are they suppressed? Because of doubt, of fear of failure, of procrastination, of putting things off till the morrow. "Straight from a mighty bow this truth is driven: They fail, and they alone, who have not striven."

Tomorrow you will live, you always cry;
In what far country does this morrow lie,
That 'tis so mighty long ere it arrive?
Beyond the Indies does this morrow live?'
Tis so far fetched, this morrow, that I fear
'Twill be both very old and very dear.
Tomorrow I will live, the fool does say;
Today itself's too late; the wise lived yesterday."

—ABRAHAM COWLEY

"To begin," said Ausonms, "is to be half done." "Greatly begin!" wrote another sage. "Though thou have time for but a line, be that sublime." And the Easterners have a proverb that the road of a thousand miles begins with one step.

So make your start, and don't allow any thought of failure to stop you. Have faith —if not in yourself—then In the Creative Force working through you. Many a splendid work has been lost to mankind because the faith of its originator was not strong enough to release the Creative Force that would have enabled him to make his dream come true.

Remember that you cannot talk failure, or think failure, and reap success. You'll never reach the top of the ladder if doubt and fear and procrastination make you hesitate to put your foot on the first rung.

There is a Power working through you that can accomplish any aim you may aspire to. But to energize that power, you must harness it up with Faith. You must have the will to believe, the courage to aspire, and the profound conviction that success is possible to anyone who works for it persistently and believingly.

Three hundred and forty years ago, there sailed from Spain the mightiest fleet the world had ever known, Spanish galleasses, Portuguese caracks, Florentine caravels, huge hulks from other countries—floating fortresses, mounting tier upon tier of mighty cannon—140 great ships in all, manned to the full with sailors and soldiers and gentlemen adventurers.

The treasure of the Incas, the Plunder of the Aztec, had gone into the building and outfitting of this vast Armada. No wonder Spain looked upon it as invincible. No wonder England feared it. For this was the Armada that was to invade England and carry fire and sword through town and countryside. This was the Armada that was to punish these impudent Britons for the "piratical" raids of Sir Francis Drake, Morgan and all those hardy seamen who had dared death and slavery to pull down treasure ships on the Spanish Main.

The iron hand of Philip II of Spain rested heavily upon the Netherlands. It dominated all of Europe. Now he confidently looked forward to the time when England, too, would groan beneath its weight.

But he reckoned without one thing—faith! He put in charge of this Invincible Armada, the Duke of Medina Sidonia, a man who had no faith in himself, no faith in his ability, no faith in his men. And when he did that, he blunted the point of every spike; he dulled the cutting edge of every sword; he took the mightiest naval weapon ever forged, and deliberately drew its sting.

Is that putting it too strongly? Just listen. Here is the letter the Duke wrote to the King, upon being notified of his appointment to the command:

"My health is bad and from my small experience of the water I know that I am always seasick...The expedition is on such a scale and the object is of such high importance that the person at the head of it ought to understand navigation and sea fighting, and I know nothing of either...The Adelantado of Castile would do better than I. The Lord would help him, he is a good Christian and has fought in naval battles. If you send me, depend upon it, I shall have a bad account to render of my trust."

He had everything to succeed with—everything but faith in himself. He expected failure—and disastrous failure met him at every turn.

One hundred and forty mighty ships—the greatest ever built. And England, to meet that splendid Armada, had only 30 small ships of war and a few merchantmen outfitted and manned by private gentlemen. Yet England, while alarmed, was yet courageous and hopeful. For had not England Sir Francis Drake?

And Lord Charles Howard? And a dozen other mighty fighters who had met and bested the Spaniards a score of times on the Spanish Main? And could they not do the same again?

So said England, believing in her leaders. And her leaders echoed that sentiment. Are not English sailors the hardiest seamen and finest fighters afloat? they asked. And believed in their men.

The English had 30 or 40 little ships against the Spaniards' 140 mighty men-of-war. The English had scarce two days' powder aboard—so penurious was their Queen—while the Spanish were outfitted with everything a ship-of-war could ask.

But Howard and Drake were not depending upon any Queen to fight their battles. They were not worrying about the size of the enemy. They were thinking— "There are the Spaniards. Here are we. We have fought them and whipped them a dozen times before. We can do it now. So let's get at them!"

They went out expecting victory. And victory met them at every turn.

From the Lizard in Cornwall to Portland, where Don Pedro de Valdes and his mighty ship were left; from Portland to Calais, where Spain lost Hugo de Moncado with the galleys which he captured; from Calais, out of sight of England, around Scotland and Ireland, beaten and shuffled together, that mighty Armada was chased, until finally the broken remnants drifted back to Spain.

With all their vast squadron, they had not taken one ship or bark of England. With all those thousands of soldiers, they had not landed one man but those killed or taken prisoner.

Three-fourths of their number lost or captured, their mighty fleet destroyed. And why? Because one man lacked faith. Spanish soldiers were proving on a dozen fields that no braver fighters lived anywhere. The "Spanish Square" had withstood infantry, cavalry, artillery—then carried all before it. Yet these same soldiers, afloat in their huge fortresses, were utterly defeated by less than a fourth their number.

And the reason? Because they were a spear without a head—an army without a leader—riches and power without faith. Was ever a better example of the power of belief?

Men go all through life like the Duke of Medina Sidonia—looking ever for the dark side of things, expecting trouble at every turn—and usually finding it. It is really lack of courage—courage to try for great things, courage to dare disappointment and ridicule to accomplish a worthy end. Have you ever sat in a train and watched another train passing you? You can look right on through its windows to the green fields and pleasant vistas beyond. Or you can gaze at the partitions between the windows and see nothing but their dingy drabness. So it is with everything in life. You can look for the good, the joyful and happy—and not merely see only these but manifest them in your daily life. Or you can look for trouble, for sickness and sorrow—and find them awaiting you around every corner.

Pessimists call this the "Pollyanna Age" and ridicule such ideas as this. But ridicule or not, it works—in one's personal life as well as in business—and thousands can testify to its efficacy.

Perhaps one of the best examples of the difference that outlook makes is in the lives of Emerson and Thoreau. Emerson's philosophy of living can best be expressed in his own words—"Nerve us with incessant affirmatives. Don't bark against the bad, but chant the beauties of the good." And his tranquil and serene life reflected that attitude throughout.

Thoreau, on the other hand, was constantly searching out and denouncing evil. With motives every whit as high as Emerson's, he believed in attacking the problem from the opposite angle, with the result that he was constantly in hot water, yet accomplished not a tenth of the good that Emerson did. Like the man in d'Annunzio's play, LA CITTA MORTA—"Fascinated by the tombs, he forgot the beauty of the sky."

It is necessary at times to clean up evil conditions in order to start afresh. It is necessary to hunt out the source of pollution in order to purify a stream. But it should be merely a means to an end. And the end should always be—not negative like the mere destruction of evil, but the positive replacing of evil with good.

If you have ever walked across a high trestle, you know that it doesn't pay to look down. That way dizziness and destruction lie. You have to look forward, picking out the ties you are going to step on ten or twenty feet ahead, if you are to progress. Life is just such a trestle. And looking downward too much is likely to make one lose his balance, stumble and fall. You must gaze ever forward if you are to keep your perspective.

There's a little poem by Edgar Guest that exemplifies the idea:

"Somebody said that it couldn't be done,

48

But he with a chuckle replied
That 'maybe it couldn't,' but he would be one
Who wouldn't say so till he'd tried.
So he buckled right in with the trace of a grin
On his face. If he worried he hid it.
He started to sing as he tackled the thing
That couldn't be done, AND HE DID IT."

Most of the world's progress has been made by just such men as that. Men like Watt, who didn't know that steam could not be made to accomplish any useful purpose, and so invented the steam engine. Men like Fulton, who didn't know that it was foolish to try to propel a boat with wheels—and so invented the steamboat. Men like Bell, Edison, Wright, who didn't know how foolish it was to attempt the impossible—and so went ahead and did it.

"For God's sake, give me the young man who has brains enough to make a fool of himself!" cried Stevenson. And when they succeed, the whole world echoes that cry.

There is no limit upon you—except the limit you put upon yourself. You are like the birds—your thoughts can fly across all barriers, unless you tie them down or cage them or clip their wings by the limitations you put upon them.

There is nothing that can defeat you—except yourself. You are one with the Father. And the Father knows everything you will ever need to know on any subject.

Why then, try to repress any right desire, any high ambition? Why not put behind it every ounce of energy, every bit of enthusiasm, of which you are capable? Mahomet established a larger empire than that of Rome on nothing but enthusiasm. And Mahomet was but a poor camel-driver. What then can you not do?

Men repress their power for good, their capacity for success, by accepting suggestions of inferiority; by their timidity or self-consciousness; by fear; by conservatism. Never mind what others think of you. It is what you think that counts. Never let another's poor opinion of you influence your decisions. Rather, resolve to show him how unfounded is his opinion.

People thought so poorly of Oliver Cromwell that he could not win permission to emigrate to the Colonies. When he raised his regiment of cavalry that later won the name of "Ironsides" because of its practical invincibility, the old soldiers and the dandies of the day laughed at it. Seldom had a lot of more awkward-looking countrymen been gathered together.

Any soldier might have trained them. But the thing that made them invincible, the thing that enabled them to ride over and through all the legions of King Charles, was not their training, but their fervent belief in the justice of their cause, in their leader and in their God.

"Hymn-singing hypocrites," their enemies called them. But here were no hypocrites. Here were men who were animated by a common faith that God was with them as with the Israelites of old—and that with God on their side, nothing could withstand them. That was the faith of Cromwell. And he instilled that faith into every man in his regiment.

And while Cromwell lived to keep that faith alive, nothing *did* withstand them. They made the man who was not good enough to emigrate to America, Ruler of England!

Nothing worthwhile ever has been accomplished without faith. Nothing worthwhile ever will. Why do so many great organizations go to pieces after their founder's death? Why do they fail to outlive him by more than a few years? Because the ones who take up his work lack the forward look, the faith, to carry on. His idea was one of service—theirs is to continue paying dividends. His thought was to build ever greater and greater—theirs to hold what he won.

"The best defensive is a strong offensive." You can't just hold your own. You can't stand still. You've got to go forward—or backward. Which is it with you? If forward, then avoid the pessimist as you would the plague. Enthusiasm, optimism, may make mistakes—but it will learn from them and progress. Pessimism, conservatism, caution, will die of dry rot, if it is not sooner lost in the forward march of things.

So be an optimist. Cultivate the forward look.

"The Optimist and Pessimist,
The difference is droll,
The Optimist sees the doughnut,
The Pessimist—the hole!"

The good is always there—if you look for it hard enough. But you must look for it. You can't be content to take merely what happens to come into your line of vision. You have got to refuse to accept anything short of good. Disclaim it! Say it is not yours. Say it—*and believe it*. Then keep a-seeking—and the first thing you know, the good you have been seeking will be found to have been right under your nose all the time.

What is the backbone of all business? Credit. And what is credit but faith—faith in your fellowman—faith in his integrity—faith in his willingness and his ability to give you a square deal?

What do you base credit-faith upon? Upon hearsay—upon what your prospective customer has done for others, his promptness in paying them, his willingness to cooperate with them. In many cases you have never seen him—you can't be certain of your own personal knowledge that such a person exists—but you believe in him, you have FAITH. And having faith, your business grows and prospers.

If you can have such faith in a man you have never seen, as to trust large portions of your earthly goods in his hands, can you not put a little trust in the Father, too?

True, you have not seen Him—but you have far greater proof of His being than of that of your customer thousands of miles away. You have far greater proof of His reliability, of His regard for you, of His ability and His willingness at all times to come to your assistance in any right way you may ask. You don't need money with Him. You don't need high standing in your community. You don't need credit.

What is it makes a successful salesman? Faith in his house. Faith in the goods he is selling. Faith In the service they will render his customers. Faith In himself. Have you faith in your "house"—in your Father—in the manifold gifts He offers you so freely?

Men can sell for a little while solely on faith in their own ability, they can palm off anything that will show a profit to themselves. But they never make successful salesmen. The inevitable reaction comes. They grow cynical, lose all faith in others —and eventually lose faith in themselves as well. The successful salesman must have a fourfold faith—faith in his house, faith in his product, faith in the good it will do his customer, faith in himself. Given such a faith, he can sell anything. Given such a faith in the Father, you can do anything.

It wasn't superior courage or superior fighting ability that enabled Washington's half-trained army to beat the British. English soldiers were showing all over the world that they were second to none in fighting qualities. And the American soldiers were, for the most part, from the same sturdy stock. It was their faith in a greater Power outside themselves.

What is it differentiates the banker from the pawnbroker? Both make loans. Both require security. But where the pawn-broker must have tangible, material property that he can resell before he will lend a cent, the really great banker bases his loans on something bigger than any security that may be offered him—his faith in the borrower.

America was built on faith. Those great railroad builders who spanned the continent knew when they did it that there was not enough business immediately available to make their investment profitable for a long time to come. But they had faith—a faith that was the making of our country.

That same faith is evident on every hand today. Men erect vast factories—in the faith that the public will find need for and buy their products. They build offices, apartments, homes—in the faith that their cities will grow up to the need of them. They put up public utilities capable of serving twice the number of people in their territories—in the faith that the demand will not only grow with the population, but the availability of the supply will help to create new demands.

Faith builds cities and businesses and men. In fact, everything of good, everything constructive in this old world of ours is based on faith. So if you have it not, *grow it*—as the most important thing you can do. And if you have it, *tend it*, water it, cultivate it—for it is the most important thing in life.

"When nothing seems to help, I go and look at a stonecutter hammering away at his rock, perhaps a hundred times without as much as a crack showing in it. Yet at the hundred and first blow, it will split in two, and I know it was not that blow that did it, but all that had gone before."—J. A. RIIS. S.

CHAPTER 5

TALISMAN

"Like the waves of the sea are the ways of fate. As we voyage along through life. 'Tis the set of the soul which decides its goal and not the calm or the strife."

—ELLA WHEELER WILCOX

WHAT IS THE ETERNAL QUESTION which stands up and looks you and every sincere man squarely in the eye every morning?

"How can I better my condition?" That is the real life question which confronts you, and will haunt you every day until you solve it.

The answer to that question lies first in remembering that the great business of life is thinking. Control your thoughts and you mold circumstance.

Just as the first law of gain is desire, so the first essential to success is FAITH. Believe that you have—see the thing you want as an existent fact—and anything you can rightly wish for is yours. Belief is "the substance of things hoped for, the evidence of things not seen."

You have seen men, inwardly no more capable than yourself, accomplish the seemingly impossible. You have seen others, after years of hopeless struggle, suddenly win their most cherished dreams. And you've often wondered, "What is the power that gives new life to their dying ambitions, that supplies new impetus to their jaded desires, that gives them a new start on the road to success?"

That power is belief—*faith*. Someone, something, gave them a new belief in themselves and a new faith in their power to win—and they leaped ahead and wrested success from seemingly certain defeat.

Do you remember the picture Harold Lloyd was in some years ago, showing a country boy who was afraid of his shadow? Every boy in the countryside bedeviled him. Until one day his grandmother gave him a talisman that she assured him his grandfather had carried through the Civil War and which, so she said, had the property of making its owner invincible. Nothing could hurt him, she told him, while he wore this talisman. Nothing could stand up against him. He believed her. And the next time the bully of the town started to cuff him around, he wiped up the earth with him. And that was only the start. Before the year was out he had made a reputation as the most daring soul in the community.

Then, when his grandmother felt that he was thoroughly cured, she told him the truth—that the "talisman" was merely a piece of old junk she'd picked up by the roadside—that she knew all he needed was *faith in himself,* belief that he could do these things.

Stories like that are common. It is such a well-established truth that you can do only what you think you can, that the theme is a favorite one with authors. I remember reading a story years ago of an artist—a mediocre sort of artist—who was visiting the field of Waterloo and happened upon a curious lump of metal half-buried in the dirt, which so attracted him that he picked it up and put it in his pocket. Soon thereafter he noticed a sudden increase in confidence, an absolute faith in himself, not only as to his own chosen line of work, but in his ability to handle any situation that might present itself. He painted a great picture—just to show that he *could* do it. Not content with that, he visioned an empire with Mexico as its basis, actually led a revolt that carried all before it— until one day he lost his talisman. Then the bubble burst.

It is your own belief in yourself that counts. It is the consciousness of dominant power within you that makes all things attainable. *You can do anything you think you can.* This knowledge is literally the gift of the gods, for through it you can solve every human problem. It should make of you an incurable optimist. It is the open door to welfare. *Keep it open*—by expecting to gain everything that is right.

You are entitled to every good thing. Therefore expect nothing but good. Defeat does not need to follow victory. You don't have to "knock wood" every time you congratulate yourself that things have been going well with you. Victory should follow victory.

Don't limit your channels of supply. Don't think that riches or success must come through some particular job or some rich uncle. It is not for you to dictate to the Creative Force the means through which it shall send Its gifts to you. There are millions of channels through which It can reach you. Your part is to impress upon Mind your need, your earnest desire, your boundless belief in the resources and the willingness of the Creative Force to help you. Plant the seed of desire. Nourish it with a clear visualization of the ripened fruit. Water it with sincere faith. But leave the means to the Creative Force.

Open up your mind. Clear out the channels of thought. Keep yourself in a state of receptivity. Gain a mental attitude in which you are constantly expecting good. You have the fundamental right to all good, you know. "According to your faith, be it unto you."

The trouble with most of us is that we are mentally lazy. It is so much easier to go along with the crowd than to break trail for ourselves. But the great discoverers, the great inventors, the great geniuses in all lines have been men who dared to break with tradition, who defied precedent, who believed that there is no limit to what Mind can do—and who stuck to that belief until their goal was won, in spite of all the sneers and ridicule of the wiseacres and the "It-can't-be-doners."

Not only that, but they were never satisfied with achieving just one success. They knew that the first success is like the first olive out of the bottle. All the others come out the more easily for it. They realized that they were a part of the Creative Force and Intelligence of the Universe, and that the part shares all the properties of the whole. And that realization gave them the faith to strive for any right thing, the knowledge that the only limit upon their capabilities was the limit of their desires. Knowing that, they couldn't be satisfied with any ordinary success. They had to keep on and on and on.

Edison didn't sit down and fold his hands when he gave us the talking machine, or the electric light. These great achievements merely opened the way to new fields of accomplishment.

Open up the channels between your mind and the Creative Force, and there is no limit to the riches that will come pouring in. Concentrate your thoughts on the particular thing you are most interested in, and ideas in abundance will come flooding down, opening up a dozen ways of winning the goal you are striving for.

But don't let one success—no matter how great—satisfy you. The Law of Life, you know, is the Law of Growth. You can't stand still. You must go forward—or be passed by.

Complacency—self-satisfaction—is the greatest enemy of achievement. You must keep looking forward. Like Alexander, you must be constantly seeking new worlds to conquer. Depend upon it, the power will come to meet the need. There is no such thing as failing powers, if we look to the Creative Force for our source of supply. The only failure of mind comes from worry and fear—and disuse.

William James, the famous psychologist, taught that—"The more mind does, the more it can do." For ideas release energy. You can do more and better work than you have ever done. You can know more than you know now. You know from your own experience that under proper mental conditions of joy or enthusiasm, you can do three or four times the work without fatigue that you can ordinarily. Tiredness is more boredom than actual physical fatigue. You can work almost indefinitely when the work is a pleasure.

You've seen sickly persons, frail persons, who couldn't do an hour's light work without exhaustion, suddenly buckle down when heavy responsibilities were thrown upon them, and grow strong and rugged under the load. Crises not only draw upon the reserve power you have but they help to create new power.

It Couldn't be Done

It may be that you have been deluded by the thought of incompetence. It may be that you have been told so often that you cannot do certain things that you've come to believe you can't. Remember that success or failure is merely a state of mind. Believe you cannot do a thing—and you can't. Know that you can do it—and you will. You must *see yourself doing it.*

"If you think you are beaten, you are; If you think you dare not, you don't; If you'd like to win, but you think you can't, It's almost a cinch you won't;

> *If you think you'll lose, you've lost,*
> *For out in the world you'll find*
> *Success begins with a fellow's will—*
> *It's all in the state of mind.*

Full man a race is lost, Ere even a race is run, And many a coward fails Ere even his work's begun.

> *Think big, and your deeds will grow,*
> *Think small and you fall behind,*
> *Think that you can, and you will;*
> *It's all in the state of mind.*

If you think you are outclassed, you are; You've got to think high to rise; You've got to be sure of yourself before You can ever win a prize.

Life's battle doesn't always go To the stronger or faster man; But sooner or later, the man who wins Is the fellow who thinks he can."

There's a vast difference between a proper understanding of one's own ability and a determination to make the best of it—and offensive egotism. It is absolutely necessary for every man to believe in himself, before he can make the most of himself. All of us have something to sell. It may be our goods, it may be our abilities, it may be our services. You've got to believe in yourself to make your buyer take stock in you at par and accrued interest. You've got to feel the same personal solicitude over a customer lost, as a revivalist over a backslider, and hold special services to bring him over into the fold. You've got to get up every morning with determination, if you're going to go to bed that night with satisfaction.

There's mighty sound sense in the saying that all the world loves a booster. The one and only thing you have to win success with is MIND. For your mind to function at its highest capacity, you've got to be charged with good cheer and optimism. No one ever did a good piece of work while in a negative frame of mind. Your best work is always done when you are feeling happy and optimistic.

And a happy disposition is the *result*—not the *cause*—of happy, cheery thinking. Health and prosperity are the *results* primarily of optimistic thoughts. You make the pattern. If the impress you have left on the world about you seems faint and weak, don't blame fate—blame your pattern! You will never cultivate a brave, courageous demeanor by thinking cowardly thoughts. You cannot gather figs from thistles. You will never make your dreams come true by choking them with doubts and fears. You've got to put foundations under your air castles, foundations of UNDERSTANDING AND BELIEF. Your chances of success in any undertaking can always be measured by your BELIEF in yourself.

Are your surroundings discouraging? Do you feel that if you were in another's place success would be easier? Just bear in mind that your real environment is within you. All the factors of success or failure are in your inner world. You make that inner world—and through it your outer world. You can choose the material from which to build it. If you've not chosen wisely in the past, you can choose again now the material you want to rebuild it. The richness of life is within you. No one has failed so long as he can begin again.

> *"For yesterday is but a dream,*
> *And tomorrow is only a vision.*
> *And today well-lived makes*
> *Every yesterday a dream of happiness,*
> *And every tomorrow a vision of hope."*

Start right in and *do* all the things you feel you have it in you to do. Ask permission of no man. Concentrating your thought upon any proper undertaking will make its achievement possible. Your belief that you can do the thing gives your thought forces their power. Fortune waits upon you. Seize her boldly, hold her—and she is yours. She belongs rightfully to you. But if you cringe to her, if you go up to her doubtfully, timidly, she will pass you by in scorn. For she is a fickle jade who must be mastered, who loves boldness, who admires confidence. Remember, you can have what you want if you will use what you have now. You can do what you want if you will do what there is to do right now. Take the first step, and your mind will mobilize all its forces to your aid. But the first essential is that you *begin.* Once the battle is started, all that is within and without you will come to your assistance, if you attack in earnest and meet each obstacle with resolution. But you have to start things. As the poet so well expresses it:

> *"Then take this honey from the bitterest cup,*
> *There is no failure save in giving up—*
> *No real fall so long as one still tries—*
> *For seeming setbacks make the strongman wise*
> *There's no defeat, in truth, save from within:*
> *Unless you're beaten there, you're sure to win."*

The men who have made their mark in this world all had one trait in common—*they believed in themselves!* "But," you may say, "how can I believe in myself when I have never yet done anything worthwhile, when everything I put my hand to seems to fail?" You can't, of course. That is, you couldn't if you had to depend upon your conscious mind alone. But just remember what One far greater than you said—"I can of mine own self do nothing. The Father that is within me—He doeth the works."

That same "FATHER" is within you, and back of Him and of you is all the Creative Force in the universe. It is by knowing that He is in you, and that through Him you can do anything that is right, that you can acquire the belief in yourself which is so necessary. Certainly the Mind that imaged the heavens and the earth and all that they contain has all wisdom, all power, all abundance. With this Mind to call upon, you know there is no problem too difficult to undertake. The *knowing* of this is the first step, *Faith,* but as Emerson expressed it in the modern manner: "He who learns and learns, and yet does not what he knows, is like the man who plows and plows, yet never sows." So go on to the next step. Decide on the one thing you want most from life, no matter what it may be. There is no limit, you know, to Mind.

Visualize this thing that you want. See it, feel it, BELIEVE in it. Make your mental blueprint, and *begin to build!* And not merely a mental blueprint, but make an actual picture of it, if you can. Cut out pictures from magazines that symbolize what you want. Paste them on a large sheet of paper and pin them up where you can see them often. You'll be surprised how such pictures help you to form the mental mold, and how quickly the Creative Force will take shape in that mold.

Suppose some people DO laugh at your idea. Suppose Reason does say—"It can't be done!" People laughed at Galileo. They laughed at Henry Ford. Reason contended for countless ages that the earth was flat. Reason said—or so numerous automotive engineers argued—that the Ford motor wouldn't run. But the earth is round—and some millions of Fords did run—and are running.

Let us start right now putting into practice some of these truths that you have learned. What do you want most of life right now? Take that one desire, concentrate on it, impress it upon your subconscious mind in every way you can, particularly with pictures. Visualizing what you want is essential, and pictures make this visualizing easier.

Psychologists have discovered that the best time to make suggestions to your subconscious mind is just before going to sleep, when the senses are quiet and the attention is lax. So let us take your desire and suggest it to your subconscious mind tonight. The two prerequisites are the earnest DESIRE, and an intelligent, understanding, BELIEF. Someone has said, you know, that education is three-fourths encouragement, and the encouragement is the suggestion that the thing can be done.

You know that you can have what you want, if you want it badly enough and can believe in it earnestly enough. So tonight, just before you drop off to sleep, concentrate your thought on this thing that you most desire from life. BELIEVE that you have it. SEE it in your mind's eye, and see YOURSELF possessing it. FEEL yourself using it.

Do that every night until you ACTUALLY DO BELIEVE that you have the thing you want. When you reach that point, YOU WILL HAVE IT!

"Do you accept the Power within, Or do you say — 'Tomorrow, Or after that, I will begin,' And try from time to time to borrow Sweet, precious moments, quickly sped, On futile paths by error led?"

Our God has willed a legacy To all of those believing. So why not change your 'it might be' To just 'I am receiving A guiding hand in every task, And full returns for all I ask.'

Do you desire success to win? Humbly accept the Power within."

—JOHN GRAHAM

CHAPTER 6

THE PERFECT PATTERN

IN Chapter 4, we quoted Baudouin to show how a person can hypnotize himself into health, happiness, success.

This is not as foolish as it sounds, for self-hypnosis is nothing more nor less than deep concentration, and it is a well-known fact that we go in the direction of our thoughts. What we long for, or dread or fear—that we are headed towards.

You see, man is inseparable from the Creative Force. God has incarnated Himself in man, and God is dynamic—not static. He cannot be shut up. He must be expressed in one way or another. We put His power into all that we do—whether towards failure or success.

How then can we use this Creative Power for good? How can we put it into our efforts toward success?

First, by convincing ourselves that we ARE successful, that we are on the road to riches or health or power. We must "believe that we receive." And the quickest, easiest, surest way to do this is through repetition. It is now generally known and accepted that one comes to believe whatever one repeats to oneself sufficiently often, whether the statement be true or false. It comes to be the dominating thought in one's mind.

Such thoughts, when mixed with a strong feeling of desire or emotion, become a magnet which attracts from all about similar or related thoughts. They attract a host of their relatives, which they add to their own magnetic power until they become the dominating, motivating master of the individual.

Then the second law begins to work. All impulses of thought have a tendency to clothe themselves in their physical equivalent. In other words, if the dominating thought in your mind is riches, that thought will tend to draw to you opportunities for riches that you never dreamed of. Just as the magnet attracts iron, so will you attract money and ways of making more money. Or if health be your dominating thought, ways and means of winning new health and strength will come to you. The same is true of love, of happiness, of anything you may greatly desire of life.

61

On the other hand, if you fill your mind with fear, doubt and unbelief in your ability to use the forces of Infinite Intelligence, these in turn will become your dominating thought and form the pattern for your life.

You will be lifted up, or pulled down, according to the pattern of your thought. There are no limitations upon the Creative Force working through you. The limitations are all in you, and they are all self-imposed. Riches and poverty are equally the offspring of your thought.

So if you desire anything of good, the first and most important thing you must do is to develop your faith that *you can have that good*. Faith, like any other state of mind, can be induced by suggestion, by repetition. Tell yourself often enough that you HAVE faith, and you will have it, for any thought that is passed on to the subconscious often enough and convincingly enough is finally accepted, and then translated into its physical equivalent by the most practical method available.

You remember the story of the king who felt that his child, if brought up in the court, would be spoiled by overmuch attention. So he put him in the family of an honest peasant, and had him raised as the peasant's own child. The boy had all the power, all the riches of the kingdom at his disposal—yet he knew it not. He was a great prince, yet because he knew nothing of it, he worked and lived as a lowly peasant.

Most of us are like that young prince, in that we are ignorant of our Divine parentage. We know nothing of the power that is ours, so we get no good from it. God is working through us, and there is nothing He cannot do, yet because we know nothing of Him, we are powerless.

There is no such thing as a human nobody. All have the Divine spark in them, all can kindle it into a glowing flame through faith. People let themselves be hypnotized by fear and anxiety, fear of poverty, of failure, of disease. They continually visualize these, and thus make them their dominant thought, using it as a magnet to draw these things to them.

Whatever form your thoughts and beliefs take, the Creative Force working through you uses as a mold in which to form your life and your surroundings. If you want to be strong, think of yourself as perfect. If you want to be prosperous, think not of debts and lacks, but of riches and opportunity. We go in the direction of our dominating thought. It strikes the keynote of our life song.

"The chief characteristic of the religion of the future," wrote Dr. Eliot, "will be man's inseparableness from the great Creative Force." We are in partnership with the Fountain Head of all good.

Emerson says that man is weak when he looks for help outside himself. It is only as he throws himself unhesitatingly upon the Creative Force within himself that he finds the springs of success, the power that can accomplish all things. It is only when he realizes that all outside help amounts to nothing compared with the tremendous forces working through him that he stands erect and begins to work miracles.

Nearly every man has a habit of looking back and saying—"If I had that period of my life to live over again, if I could go back and take advantage of the chance at fortune I had then, I'd be rich and successful today."

Yet a year from now, or five or ten years from now, most of you who read this will be saying the same thing of today.

Why? Because your future depends upon the foundations you are digging NOW. Yesterday is gone. There is no recalling it. And tomorrow has not come. The only time you have to work with is right now, and whether you will go up or down tomorrow, whether you will be rich or a failure, depends upon your thoughts today.

It took mankind thousands of years to learn how to control matter, how to provide comfort and safety and some degree of financial security. It has taken less than a generation to learn how to control one's own future. The knowledge is so new that most people are not yet aware of it. As David Seabury put it in his book—"They know that science and mechanics have made over the face of the earth. They do not know that psychology and its kindred sciences are making a like change in man's handling of his own nature."

Do you know why so few people succeed in life? Because it is so EASY that most people cannot believe in the methods that really make men successful. They prefer to look upon success as something arduous, something practically impossible for them to attain—and by looking upon it that way, make it so for themselves.

YOU CAN HAVE WHAT YOU WANT—if you know how to plant the seeds of it in your thought. To know that is the most important thing that anyone can learn. It is not fate that bars your path. It is not lack of money or opportunity. It is yourself —your attitude towards life. Change it—and you change all.

Ask yourself this important question: Are you a victim of self-pity? Are you embittered at life and at those more successful than yourself? Do you think fortune has played you a scurvy trick? Or are you cheerfully, steadfastly, confidently working out ways of meeting and bettering the situations that life presents to you?

Most people will dodge that question. They are more concerned in defending their ego and putting the blame for their failures on something outside themselves than they are in getting ahead. Failure comes from the inside first. It cannot be forced upon a resolute, dauntless soul.

How about YOU? Will you give yourself an honest answer to this important question—"Are you a victim of self-pity?"

Think of the times when you have yearned for a future—when you have grown impatient with the barriers that seemed to hold you down—when you have heard of the success of some acquaintance whom you knew to be inwardly no more capable than yourself. Are you willing to keep on wishing and *envying* and looking to the future for your success? Or will you start that success in the only time that will ever be yours to work with—the everlasting NOW?

Remember what Emerson told us: "There is one Mind common to all individual men. Every man is an inlet to the same and to ALL of the same. He that is once admitted to the right of reason is a freeman of the whole estate. What Plato has thought, he may think; what a Saint has felt, he may feel; what has at any time befallen any man, he can understand. Who hath access to this Universal Mind is a party to all that is or can be done; for this is the only and sovereign agent—of this Universal Mind each individual is one more incarnation."

The Creative Force of the Universe is working through you. You can be as great an outlet for IT as anyone who has ever lived. You have only to provide the mold in which it is to take shape, and that mold is formed by your thoughts. What is your dominant desire? What do you want most? *Believe in it*—and you can have it. Make it your dominating thought, magnetize your mind with it, and you will draw to you everything you need for its accomplishment.

"There is not a dream that may not come true," wrote Arthur Symons, "if we have the energy which makes or chooses our own fate. We can always in this world get what we want, if we *will* it intensely and persistently enough. So few people succeed because so few can conceive a great end and work towards it without deviating and without tiring. But we all know that the man who works for money day and night gets rich; and the man who works day and night for no matter what kind of material power, gets the power. It is only the dreams of those light sleepers who dream faintly that do not come true."

Knowing these things, can you ever again limit yourself, when you have such unlimited possibilities? Sure, there are times when you feel inferior. Everyone does. Just remember and realize that *you* are superior, one of the efficient few who take advantage of the Infinite Power inside them to carry you on to the heights of success.

Plato held, you remember, that in the Divine Mind are pure forms or Archetypes according to which all visible beings are made. And most of the great Mystery Schools of the older world held similar opinions. They taught growth by intent rather than by accident, a development from birth all through life towards the perfect image or Archetype of each of us that is held in Divine Mind. They visioned each of us growing into a destiny that had been imaged for him long before he was born.

Progress was movement in the direction of the perfect Archetype. Man became nobler as the interval between him and his perfect pattern grew less. To the Greeks, happiness meant peace between a man and his pattern, whereas if you lived in a manner inconsistent with your Archetype, you suffered from inharmonies of various kinds. They believed that it was not so much what you do that causes you to suffer, as it is the Inharmony between what you do and what you SHOULD DO to match your perfect pattern.

There is a perfect pattern for YOU in the Divine Mind, a perfect Archetype that you CAN match. It has perfect form, perfect intelligence, all power necessary to make your surroundings perfect. Why not make yourself like it?

You CAN! Just let your Archetype be your model. Fill your mind with thoughts of its perfection, make it your dominant thought, and you can draw to yourself whatever elements you need to manifest that perfect Image. And not merely the perfect image of yourself, but all that goes to make your surroundings and circumstances just as perfect. Remember, the only limit upon the Power working through you is the limit you impose.

Bear these facts in mind:

1 Your subconscious mind is constantly amenable to control by the power of suggestion.

2 Its power to reason deductively from given premises to correct conclusions is practically perfect.

3 It is endowed with a perfect memory.

4 It is the seat of your emotions.

5 It has the power to communicate and receive intelligence through other than the recognized channels of the senses.

"Man contains all that is needful within himself," wrote Emerson. "He is made a law unto himself. All real good or evil that can befall him must be from himself. The purpose of life seems to be to acquaint a man with himself. The highest revelation is that God is in every man."

CHAPTER 7

TO HIM THAT HATH

THE LAW OF Increase states that: "To him that hath, shall be given." To him that is using his attractive powers, shall be given everything he needs for growth and fruition. "From him that hath not, shall be taken away even that which he hath." The penalty for not using your attractive powers is the loss of them. You are demagnetized.

Sounds simple, doesn't it, yet it is the basic law of all success, all riches, all power. It is the way the whole universe is run. You live by it, whether you like it or not, or you die by it.

To many, this law seems unfair, but in this, as in all things, Nature is logical, and when you understand exactly how the law works, you will agree that it is eminently just and right.

You see, everything consists primarily of electricity—of tiny protons and electrons revolving about each other. It is of these that your body is made, it is of these that all plant life is made, it is of these that all so-called inanimate life is made. Wherein, then, is the difference between all these forms of life? Largely in their RATE OF MOTION!

Remember this: Starting with the individual cell in your mother's womb, you attract to yourself only those elements that are identical in quality and character with yourself, and that are revolving at the same rate of speed. Your selective ability is such that you are able to pick such material as will preserve your quality and identity.

This is true of your body, of your circumstances, of your environment. Like attracts like. If you are not satisfied with yourself as you are, if you want a healthier body, more attractive friends, greater riches and success, you must start at the core—within YOURSELF!

And the first essential to putting yourself in harmony with the Infinite Good all about you is to relax, to take off the brakes. For what is worry or fear or discouragement but a brake on your thinking and on the proper functioning of your organs, a slowing down of your entire rate of activity?

"Get rid of your tensions!" says the modern psychologist. By which he means— think more about the agreeable things and less about the disagreeable ones. You know how martial music stirs your pulses, wakes even the tiredest man into action. Why? Because it tends to increase the rate of motion in every cell in your body. You know how good news has often cured sick people, how sudden excitement has enabled paralyzed people to leap from their beds. Why? Because good news makes you happy, speeds up your rate of motion, even as sudden excitement stirs up the whole organism. You know how fear, hatred, and discouragement slow you down. Why? Because those feelings put a definite clamp upon your rate of motion.

Remember this: Hatred, anger, fear, worry, discouragement—all the negative emotions—not only slow down your rate of motion, and thus bring on sickness and make you old before your time, but they definitely keep the good from you. Like attracts like, and the good things you desire have a different rate of motion from these negative ones.

Love, on the other hand, attracts and binds to you the things you love. As Drummond tells us—"To love abundantly is to live abundantly, and to love forever is to live forever." And Emerson expresses the same idea—"Love and you shall be loved. All love is mathematically just, as much as the two sides of an algebraic equation."

Whate'er thou lovest, man,

That, too, become thou must;
God, if thou lovest God,
Dust, if thou lovest dust."

And that, again, is strictly logical, strictly in accord with Nature's law that like attracts like. Whatever your rate of motion, the elements of like quality with that rate of emotion will be attracted to you.

Which brings us back to the law of increase: you will see that it is not mere money or possessions that attracts more money—it is the USE to which these are put. You can't bury your talent and expect increase. You must put it to good use. It is the rate of motion that attracts increase, what the modern merchant would call the "turn-over." The oftener he turns over his stock of goods, the more money he makes on his invested capital. But if he fails to turn it over, if his goods lie dormant on his shelves, they will gather dust or mold and presently be worthless.

We see the same thing happening every day. Statistics show that of all those who inherit money, only one in seventeen dies with money; of all those possessed of fortunes at the age of 35, only 17% have them when they reach 65.

The old adage used to be—"Three generations from shirtsleeves to shirtsleeves," but the modern tempo has speeded this up until now most fortunes hardly last out a single generation. Why is this? Because of the old law of the Rate of Motion. The man who makes the money has set in motion some idea of service that has attracted riches to him. More often than not, it is the idea or the service that is important in his mind. The money is incidental, and is attracted to him with other things of good because he has set in motion an idea that is bringing good to others.

But when he dies, what happens? Too often the business is carried on solely with the thought of how much money can be made out of it. Or the business is sold, and the money put out at interest, with the sole idea of hanging on to the money in hand. Naturally its rate of movement slows down. Naturally it begins to disintegrate and its parts are gradually drawn away by the stronger forces around it, until of that fortune there is nothing left.

You see exactly the same thing in Nature. Take any seed of plant life; take an acorn, for instance. You put it in the ground—plant it. What happens? It first gives of all the elements it has within itself to put forth a shoot, which in turn shall draw from the sun and the air the elements that they have to give; and at the same time, it puts out roots to draw from the earth the moisture and other elements it needs for growth. Its top reaches upward to the sun and air, its roots burrow deeply into the ground for moisture and nourishment. Always it is reaching out. Always it is creating a vacuum, using up all the materials it has on hand, drawing to itself from all about every element it needs for growth.

Time passes. The oak tree stops growing. What happens? In that moment, its attractive power ceases. Can it then live on the elements it has drawn to itself and made a part of itself through all those years? No, indeed! The moment growth stops, disintegration starts. Its component elements begin to feel the pull of the growing plants around them. First the moisture drains out of the tree. Then the leaves fall, the bark peels off—finally the great trunk crashes down, to decay and form soil to nourish the growing plants around. Soon of that noble oak, nothing is left but the enriched soil and the well-nourished plants that have sprung from it.

The Fundamental Law of the Universe is that you must integrate or disintegrate. You must grow—or feed others who are growing. There is no standing still. You are either attracting to yourself all the unused forces about you, or you are giving your own to help build some other man's success.

"To him that hath, shall be given." To him that is using his attractive powers, shall be given everything he needs for growth and fruition. "From him that hath not, shall be taken away even that which he hath." The penalty for not using your attractive powers is the loss of them. You are demagnetized. And like a dead magnet surrounded by live ones, you must be content to see everything you have drawn to yourself taken by them, until eventually even you are absorbed by their resistless force.

That is the first and fundamental Law of the Universe. But how are you to become an Attracter? How are you to make your start? In the same way that it has been done from the beginning of time.

Go back to the first law of life. Go back to the beginning of things. You will find Nature logical in all that she does. If you want to understand how she works, study her in her simplest, most elementary forms. The principles established there hold good throughout the universe. The methods there used are used by all created things, from the simplest to the most complicated.

How, for instance, did the earliest forms of cell life, either plant or animal, get their food? By absorbing it from the waters around them. How does every cell in your body, every cell in plant or tree or animal, get its food today? In exactly the same way—by absorbing it from the lymph or water surrounding it! Nature's methods do not change. She is logical in everything. She may build more complicated organisms, she may go in for immense size or strange combinations, but she uses the same principles throughout all of life.

Now, what is Nature's principle of Increase? From the beginning of Time, it has been—*Divide—and Grow!*

That principle, like every other fundamental Law of Nature, is the same in all of life. It has remained unchanged since the first single-celled organism floated on the surface of the primordial sea. It is the fundamental Law of Increase.

Take the lowest form of cell life. How does it grow? It DIVIDES—each part grows back to its original size—then they in turn divide and grow again.

Take the highest form of cell life—MAN. The same principle works in him in exactly the same way—in fact, it is the only principle of growth that Nature knows!

How does this apply to your circumstances, to the acquisition of riches, to the winning of success?

Look up any miracle of increase in the Bible, and what do you find? First division —then increase.

When Russell Conwell was building the famous Baptist Temple in Philadelphia, his congregation was poor and greatly in need of money. Through prayer and every other means known to him, Conwell was constantly trying to help his flock.

One Sunday it occurred to him that the old Jewish custom had been, when praying to God, to first make an offering of the finest lamb of the flock, or of some other much prized possession. Then, after freely giving to God, prayer was made for His good gifts.

So instead of first praying, and then taking up the collection, as was the custom, Conwell suggested that the collection be taken first and that all who had special favors to ask of the Creator should give freely as a "Thank Offering."

A few weeks afterwards, Conwell asked that those who had made offerings on this occasion should tell their experiences. The results sounded unbelievable. One woman who had an overdue mortgage on her home found it necessary to call in a plumber the following week to repair a leak. In tearing up the boards, he uncovered a hiding place where her late father had hidden all his money—enough to pay off the mortgage and leave plenty over!

One man got a much-needed job; a servant some dresses she badly needed; a student the chance to study for his chosen vocation, while literally dozens had their financial needs met. They had complied with the law. They had sown their seed—freely—and they reaped the harvest.

Many people will tell you—"I don't see why God does not send me riches, I have prayed for them, and promised that if I get them, I will use them to do good." God enters into no bargains with man. He gives you certain gifts to start, and upon the way you use these depends whether you get more. You've got to start with what you have.

And the place to start is pointed out in a little poem by Nina Stiles:

"The land of opportunity Is anywhere we chance to be,

Just any place where people live

And need the help that we can give."

The basis of all work, all business, all manufacturing, is SERVICE. Every idea of success must start with that. Every nucleus that is to gather to itself elements of good must have as its basis service to your fellow man. Carlyle defined wealth clearly when he said that "the wealth of a man is the number of things he loves and blesses, which he is loved and blessed by."

And that is the only kind of wealth that endures. Love and blessings speed up your rate of motion, keep your nucleus active, keep it drawing to you every element of good that you need for its complete and perfect expression. They are, in effect, a constant prayer—the kind of prayer Coleridge had in mind when he wrote—

"He prayeth well who loveth well.
Both man and bird and beast.
He prayeth best who loveth best
All things both great and small;
For the dear God who loveth us,
He made and loveth all."

Remember that the word often used in the Bible to signify "prayer" means, when literally translated—"To sing a song of joy and praise." In other words, to speed up your rate of motion with joy and thanksgiving. And you have only to read the Bible to know how often the great characters of the Bible had recourse to this method.

What do *you* want from life? Speed up your rate of motion and overtake it. Is it health you want? Then start by relaxing, by letting go of all your fears and worries. In a recent article, I read: "Dr. Loring Swaim, director of a famous clinic in Massachusetts, has under observation 270 cases of arthritis which were cured when they became free from worry, fear, and resentment. He has come to the conclusion after some years that no less than 60% of his cases are caused by moral conflict."

In the *Reader's Digest* some months ago, it was stated that, "Personal worry is one of the principal causes of physical ailments which send people to hospitals. It is literally possible to worry yourself sick; in fact, the chances are better than even that if you are ill, worry is causing the symptoms."

That is not a modern discovery, by any means. In Proverbs, you will find the statement—"A merry heart causeth good healing, but a broken spirit drieth up the bones." And Plato observed 19 centuries ago—"If the head and the body are to be well, you must begin by curing the soul."

So the first essential in curing yourself of any ailment would seem to be to let go of your resentments, your worries and fears. Make peace within yourself, within your thoughts. Laugh a little; sing a little. Dance a little, if you can. Exercise speeds up your rate of motion, but it should be joyous exercise. Do something you enjoy, something that speeds up your mind as well as your muscles. Dance, if you like dancing. Swim, ride horseback, play tennis—do something exhilarating to the spirit as well as the body. Mere routine exercises that soon become a chore do little good and often are harmful. Unless you can get mental as well as physical exhilaration out of your exercise, don't bother with it at all.

Do you want money, riches? Then use what you have, no matter how little it may be. Speed up your rate of turnover, as the merchant speeds the turnover of his stocks. Money is now your stock. Use it! Pay it out joyfully for any good purpose, and as you pay it, BLESS IT! Bless it in some such wise as this:

"I bless you...and be thou a blessing; May you enrich all who touch you. I thank God for you, but I thank Him even more that there is unlimited supply where you came from. I bless that Infinite Supply. I thank God for it, and I expand my consciousness to take in as much of it as I can use...As I release this money in my hand, I know that I am opening the gates of Infinite Supply to flow through my channels and through all that are open to receive it. The Spirit is making this money attract to itself everything it needs for growth and increase. All of God's channels are open and flowing freely for me. The best in myself for the world—the best in the world for me."

There is no quicker way of speeding up your rate of motion than by giving. Give of your time, of your money, of your services—whatever you have to give. Give of that you want to see increased, for your gift is your seed, and "everything increaseth AFTER ITS KIND!"

Solomon was the richest man of his day, and he gave us the key to his riches and success when he wrote:

"There is that scattereth, and increaseth yet more. And there is that witholdeth more than is meet. The liberal soul shall be made fat, and he that watereth, shall be watered himself."

Do you want power, ability, greater skill in what you are doing? Then use what you have, use it to the greatest extent of which you are capable. The *Sunshine Bulletin* had an excellent little piece along these lines:

"There is a task for today which can be done now better than at any other time. It is today's duty. And we are writing now a judgment upon our lives by our faithfulness or unfaithfulness at the present moment.

"This moment has its own priceless value, and if wasted, it can no more be recovered than jewels that are cast into the depths of the ocean.

"Each day has its share in the making of our tomorrow; and the future will be nobler or meaner by reason of what we now do or leave undone."

What is ambition but the inner urge that speeds up your rate of motion and makes you work harder and longer and more purposefully to the end that you may accomplish something worthwhile? What is perseverance but the will to carry on in spite of all difficulties and discouragements? Given that ambition and that perseverance, there is nothing you cannot accomplish, nothing with a rate of motion so high that you cannot overtake it.

"It is in loving, not in being loved, The heart is blessed.

It is in giving, not in seeking gifts, We find our quest.

"If thou art hungry, lacking heavenly bread, Give hope and cheer. If thou art sad and wouldst be comforted, Stay sorrow's tear.

"Whatever be thy longing or thy need, That do thou give. So shall thy soul be fed, and thou indeed Shalt truly live."

—M. ELLA RUSSELL

CHAPTER 8

EVERYTHING HAS ITS PRICE

"Dear God, help me be wise enough to see That as I give so it is meted out to me! Help me to know that with my every thought The good or ill that's mine myself I've wrought!

Help me to place all blame of lack on me, Not on my fellow man, nor yet on Thee. Give me the courage, God, truly to know That as I'd reap in life thus must I sow!"

—VERAM. CRIDER

IN HIS ESSAY on Compensation, Emerson says:

"What will you have?" quoth God. "Pay for it, and take it!"

How can we buy the things we want at the counter of God? What pay can we offer?

Perhaps the answer lies in the ancient Law of Karma. Karma is Sanskrit, you know, and means "Comeback." It is one of the oldest laws known to man. It is the law of the boomerang.

In the parlance of today, it is—"Chickens come home to roost." Even in science we find it, as Newton's Third Law of Motion—"Action and reaction are equal to each other." Ella Wheeler Wilcox expressed the Law beautifully when she wrote—

"There are loyal hearts, there are spirits brave, There are souls that are pure and true; Then give to the world the best you have, And the best will come back to you.

"Give love, and love to your heart will flow, A strength in your utmost need; Have faith, and a score of hearts will show Their faith in your word and deed.

"For life is the mirror of king and slave, Tis just what you are and do, Then give to the world the best you have And the best will come back to you."

One of the best illustrations of the working of the Law lies in the two seas of Palestine, the Sea of Galilee and the Dead Sea. The Sea of Galilee contains fresh water and is alive with fish. Green trees adorn its banks and farms and vineyards spread all around it. The River Jordan flows into it, and all the little rivulets from the hills around feed its sparkling waters.

The Dead Sea, on the other hand, knows no splash of fish, has no vegetation around it, no homes, no farms or vineyards. Travelers give it a wide berth, unless forced by urgent business to use its shores. The air hangs heavy, and neither man nor beast will drink of the waters.

What makes the difference? The River Jordan empties the same good waters into both seas. So it is not the river. And it is not the soil or the country round about.

The difference lies in the fact that the Sea of Galilee gives as it receives; for every drop of water that flows into it, another flows out. Whereas the Dead Sea holds on to all it receives. Water leaves it only through evaporation and seepage. It hoards all it gets, and the result is that the water stagnates, turns salt, and is good for naught.

In all of Nature, the only known law of increase is that you must give to get. If you want to reap a harvest, you must first plant your seed. If you want to increase your strength, you must first break up the muscle cells, and stimulate them to divide and grow.

Division and growth is the way that all of life increases. Watch a single cell at work in your body, in a plant, or in any form of life. What happens? It first divides, then each half grows until it reaches its normal size, when it divides and starts growing again. Without division, there is no growth—only atrophy and decay. You must divide to grow; you must give to get.

John Bunyan knew nothing of the law of cell growth, but he expressed it just as well when he wrote—

"A man there was and they called him mad; The more he gave, the more he had."

And Moffatt had the same thought in his couplet:

"One gives away, and still he grows the richer; Another keeps what he should give, and is the poorer."

Even the thoughts we send forth return to us laden with a harvest of their kind. That which we put into our thought comes back into our own lives, because for every thought there is a response, a return of the pendulum we have started swinging. It is the Einstein doctrine of the extended line, which must return to its source.

There is no use saying you have not enough money or abilities to be worth starting with. Start with what you have and plant your seed, no matter how small and unimportant it may seem. What you have to start with can hardly be smaller than a tiny seed. If it can grow into a tree, think what your seed may grow into.

"*Do the thing* and you shall have the power," says Emerson. "But they that do not the thing have not the power. Everything has its price, and if the price is not paid —not that thing but something else is obtained. And it is impossible to get anything without its price. For any benefit received, a tax is levied. In nature, nothing can be given—all things are sold. Power to him who power exerts.

"You are not higher than your lowest thought,
Or lower than the peak of your desire.
And all existence has no wonder wrought
To which ambition may not yet aspire.
Oh man! There is no planet, sun or star
Could hold you, if you but knew what you are."

The key to power lies in using what you have, for use releases more power, just as using your muscles builds them into greater muscles, and failing to use them makes them weak and useless. "The one condition coupled with the gift of truth," Emerson tells us, "is its USE! That man shall be learned who reduces his learning to practice."

And Goethe expressed it even more strongly when he wrote—

> *"Lose this day loitering, it will be the same story*
> *Tomorrow, and the rest more dilatory;*
> *Thus indecision brings its own delays*
> *And days are lost tormenting over other days.*
> *Are you in earnest? Seize this very minute;*
> *What you can do, or dream you can, begin it;*
> *Boldness has genius, power, and magic in it;*
> *Only engage and then the mind grows heated;*
> *Begin, and then the work will be completed."*

CHAPTER 9

YESTERDAY ENDED LAST NIGHT

"I said to the man who stood at the gate of the year: 'Give me a light that I may tread safely into the unknown.' And he replied: 'Go out into the darkness and put your hand into the hand of God. That shall be to you better than a light and safer than a known way.'"

WHAT DO YOU WANT from life? Whatever it is, you can have it—and you have the word of no less an authority than God for that.

There was an article in *Unity* magazine recently that exemplified the idea so well that I quote it here:

"Let us say we are planning a business venture, or a social event, or a religious meeting, or the recovery of the sick. We are ready to pray over the situation. Now instead of futurizing our prayers and asking for something to take place tomorrow, let us imagine (imagination is an aid to the release of faith power) that everything has turned out just as we desired it. Let us write it all down as if it were all past history. Many of the Bible predictions are written in the past tense. Let us try listing our desires as if they had already been given us.

"Of course we shall want to write down a note of thanksgiving to God for all that He has given us. He has had it for us all the time or else we should not have received it. More than this, God has it for us or we could not even desire it now or picture it in our imagination.

What happens? After we have written down our desires in the past tense, read them over carefully, praised God for them, let us then put away our paper and go on about our business. It will not be long before we actually see the desired events taking place in ways so natural that we may even forget that God is answering our prayers.

"Imagination helps us to have faith, for it pictures the thing desired and helps make it real. After we have tried this experiment a few times we shall find that our imagination has increased our faith, and faith has turned to praise, and praise has opened our eyes to see what God has for us."

The habit of thanking God ahead of time for benefits about to be received has its firm basis in past experience. We can safely look upon it as a sure formula for successful prayer because the prophets used it. David always praised and thanked God when he was in trouble. Daniel was saved from the lions through the praise of God. And don't you, and everyone else, find satisfaction in being praised for a task well done?

Wrote William Law:

"If anyone could tell you the shortest, surest way to all happiness and all perfection, he must tell you to make it a rule yourself to thank and praise God for everything that happens to you. For it is certain that whatever seeming calamity happens to you, if you thank and praise God for it, you turn it into a blessing. Could you therefore work miracles, you could not do more for yourself than by this thankful spirit; for it...turns all that it touches into happiness."

And Charles Fillmore adds:

"Praise is closely related to prayer; it is one of the avenues through which spirituality expresses itself. Through an inherent law of mind, we increase whatever we praise. The whole creation responds to praise, and is glad. Animal trainers pet and reward their charges with delicacies for acts of obedience; children glow with joy and gladness when they are praised. Even vegetation grows better for those who love it. We can praise our own ability, and the very brain cells will expand and increase in capacity and intelligence, when we speak words of encouragement and appreciation to them."

So don't let anything that has happened in your life discourage you. Don't let poverty or lack of education or past failures hold you back. There is only one power—the I AM in you—and it can do anything. If in the past you have not used that power, that is too bad as far as the past is concerned, but it is not too late. You can start NOW. "Be still, and know that I AM God." What more are you waiting for? God can do for you only what you allow Him to do through you, but if you will do your part, He can use you as a channel for unlimited power and good.

The difference between failure and success is measured only by your patience and faith—sometimes by inches, sometimes by minutes, sometimes by the merest flash of time.

Take Lincoln. He went into the Black Hawk War a Captain—and came out a private. His store failed—and his surveyor's instruments, on which he depended to eke out a livelihood, were sold for part of the debts. He was defeated in his first try for the Legislature. Defeated in his first attempt for Congress. Defeated in his application for Commissioner of the General Land Office. Defeated for the Senate. Defeated for the nomination for the Vice Presidency in 1856. But did he let that long succession of defeats discourage him? Not he. He held the faith—and made perhaps the greatest President we have ever had.

Then there was Grant: He failed of advancement in the army. Failed as a farmer. Failed as a businessman. At 39, he was chopping and delivering cordwood to keep body and soul together. Nine years later he was President of the United States and had won a martial renown second in this country only to Washington's.

Search the pages of history. You will find them dotted with the names of men whom the world had given up as failures, but who held on to their faith, who kept themselves prepared—and when their chance came they were ready and seized it with both hands.

Napoleon, Cromwell, Patrick Henry, Paul Jones—these are only a few out of thousands.

When Caesar was sent to conquer Gaul, his friends found him one day in a fit of utter despondency. Asked what the matter was, he told them he had just been comparing his accomplishments with Alexander's. At his age, Alexander had conquered the entire known world—and what had Caesar done to compare with that? But he presently roused himself from his discouragement by resolving to make up as quickly as might be for his lost time. The result? He became the head of the Roman Empire.

The records of business are crowded with the names of middle-aged nobodies who lived to build great fortunes, vast institutions. No man has failed as long as he has faith in the Father, faith in the great scheme of things, faith in himself.

When Robert Bruce faced the English at the battle of Bannockburn, he had behind him years of failure, years of fruitless efforts to drive the English out of Scotland, years of heart-breaking toil in trying to unite the warring elements among the Scotch themselves. True, at the moment a large part of Scotland was in his hands, but so had it been several times before, only to be wrested from him as soon as the English brought together a large enough army.

And now in front of him stood the greatest army England had ever gathered to her banners—hardy veterans from the French provinces, all the great English nobles with their armored followers, wild Irish, Welsh bowmen—troops from all the dominions of Edward II, over 100,000 men.

To conquer whom Bruce had been able to muster but 30,000 men, brave and hardy, it is true, but lacking the training and discipline of the English.

Was Bruce discouraged? Not he. What though the English had the better archers. What though they were better armed, better trained, better disciplined. He was fighting for freedom—and he believed in himself, he believed in his men, he believed in the God of battles.

And, as always, weight, numbers, armament, proved of no avail when confronted with determination and faith. The vast English host was completely defeated and dispersed. Bruce was firmly seated upon the throne of Scotland, and never more did an invading English army cross its borders.

It matters not how many defeats you have suffered in the past, how great the odds may be against you. Bulow put it well when he said—"It's not the size of the dog In the fight that counts, so much as the size of the fight in the dog." And the size of fight in you depends upon your faith—your faith in yourself, in the Creative Force working through you and in your cause. Just remember that yesterday ended last night, and yesterday's defeats with it.

Time after time throughout the Bible we are told that the battle is not ours—but the Lord's. But like all children, we know better than our Father how our affairs should be handled, so we insist upon running them ourselves.

Is it any wonder they get so tangled as to leave us in the depths of discouragement?

When the Black Prince with his little army was penned in by Philip of France, most men would have felt discouraged. For the hosts of France seemed as numerous as the leaves on the trees, while the English were few, and mostly archers. And archers, in that day, were believed to stand no chance against such armored knights as rode behind the banners of Philip,

The French came forward in a great mass, thinking to ride right over that little band of English. But did the Black Prince give way? Not he. He showed the world that a new force had come into warfare, a force that would soon make the armored knight as extinct as the dodo. That force was the common soldier—the archer.

Just as the Scotch spearmen overthrew the chivalry of England on the field of Bannockburn, just as infantry have overthrown both cavalry and artillery in many a later battle, so did the "common men" of England—the archers—decide the fate of the French at Crecy. From being despised and looked down upon by every young upstart with armor upon his back, the "common men"—the spearmen and archers—became the backbone of every successful army. And from what looked like certain annihilation, the Black Prince by his faith in himself and his men became one of the greatest conquerors of his day.

Troubles flocked to him, but he didn't recognize them as troubles—he thought them opportunities. And used them to raise himself and his soldiers to the pinnacle of success.

There are just as many prizes in business as in war—just as many opportunities to turn seeming troubles into blessings. But those prizes go to men like the Black Prince who don't know a trouble when they meet it—who welcome it, take it to their bosoms, and get from it their greatest blessings.

What is the use of holding on to life—unless at the same time you hold on to your faith? What is the use of going through the daily grind, the wearisome drudgery— if you have given up hoping for the rewards, and unseeing, let them pass you by?

Suppose business and industry did that? How far would they get? It is simply by holding on hopefully, believingly, watchfully—as Kipling put it: "Forcing heart and nerve and sinew to serve your turn long after they are gone, and so hold on when there is nothing in you except the will which says to them: 'Hold on'"—that many a businessman has worked out his salvation.

It is not enough to work. The horse and the ox do that. And when we work without thought, without hope, we are no better than they. It is not enough to merely hold on. The poorest creatures often do that mechanically, for lack of the courage to let go.

If you are to gain the reward of your labors, if you are to find relief from your drudgery, you must hold on hopefully, believingly, confidently—knowing that the answer is in the great heart of God, knowing that the Creative Force working through you will give it to you, the moment you have prepared yourself to receive it.

It is never the gifts that are lacking. It is never the Creative Force that is backward in fulfilling our desires. It is we who are unable to see, who fail to recognize the good, because our thoughts are of discouragement and lack.

So never let yesterday's failure discourage you. As T. C. Howard wrote in *Forbes* Magazine:

"Yesterday's gone—it was only a dream; Of the past there is naught but remembrance. Tomorrow's a vision thrown on Hope's screen, A will-o'-the-wisp, a mere semblance.

"Why mourn and grieve over yesterdays ills And paint memory's pictures with sorrow? Why worry and fret—for worrying kills—
Over things that won't happen tomorrow?

"Yesterday's gone—it has never returned—
Peace to its ashes, and calm;
Tomorrow no human has ever discerned,
Still hope, trust, and faith are its balm.

"This moment is all that I have as my own,
To use well, or waste, as I may; But I know that my future depends alone On the way that I live today.

"This moment my past and my future I form;
I may make them whatever I choose
By the deeds and the acts that I now perform,
By the words and thoughts that I use.

"So I fear not the future nor mourn o'er the past
For I do all I'm able today,
Living each present moment as though 'twere my last; Perhaps it is! Who
knows! Who shall say?"

"Duty and today are ours," a great man once wrote. "Results and the future belong to God." And wise old Emerson echoed the same thought. "All that I have seen," he said, "teaches me to trust the Creator for all I have not seen." In short, a good daily prayer might be one I read in a magazine recently—"Lord, I will keep on rowing. YOU steer the boat!"

Easy enough to say, perhaps you are thinking, but you never knew such disaster as has befallen me. I am broken down with sickness, or crippled by accident, or ruined financially, or something else equally tragic. Shakespeare wrote the answer to your case when he told us—"When Fortune means to man most good, she looks upon him with a threatening eye."

In the town of Enterprise, Ala., there is a monument erected by its citizens for services done them. And you could never guess to whom it is dedicated. To the Boll Weevil!

In olden days, the planters living thereabouts raised only cotton. When cotton boomed, business boomed. When the cotton market was off—or the crop proved poor—business suffered correspondingly.

Then came the Boll Weevil. And instead of merely a poor crop, left no crop at all. The Boll Weevil ruined everything. Debt and discouragement were all it left in its wake.

But the men of that town must have been lineal descendants of those hardy fighters who stuck to the bitter end in that long-drawn-out struggle between North and South. They got together and decided that what their town and their section needed was to stop putting all their eggs into one basket.

Instead of standing or falling by the cotton crop, diversify their products! Plant a dozen different kinds of crops. Even though one did fail, even though the market for two or three products happened to be off, the average would always be good.

Correct in theory, certainly. But, as one of their number pointed out, how were the planters to start? They were over their heads in debt already. It would take money for seeds and equipment, to say nothing of the fact that they had to live until the new crops came in.

So the townsfolk raised the money—at the Lord only knows what personal sacrifices—and financed the planters.

The result? Such increased prosperity that they erected a monument to the Boll Weevil, and on it they put this inscription:

"In profound appreciation of the Boll Weevil, this monument is erected by the citizens of Enterprise, Coffee Co., Ala."

Many a man can look back and see where some Boll Weevil—some catastrophe that seemed tragic at the time—was the basis of his whole success in life. Certainly that has been the case with one man I know.

When he was a tot of five, he fell into a fountain and all but drowned. A passing workman pulled him out as he was going down for the last time. The water in his lungs brought on asthma, which, as the years went on, kept growing worse and worse, until the doctors announced that death was only a matter of months. Meantime, he couldn't run, he couldn't play like other children; he couldn't even climb the stairs!

A sufficiently tragic outlook, one would say. Yet out of it came the key to fortune and success.

Since he could not play with the other children, he early developed a taste for reading. And as it seemed so certain that he could never do anything worthwhile for himself, what more natural than that he should long to read the deeds of men who had done great things. Starting with the usual boy heroes, he came to have a particular fondness for true stories of such men as Lincoln, Edison, Carnegie, Hill and Ford—men who started out as poor boys, without any special qualifications or advantages, and built up great names solely by their own energy and grit and determination.

Eventually he cured himself completely of his asthma—but that is another story.

The part that is pertinent to this tale is that from the time he could first read until he was seventeen, he was dependent for amusement almost entirely upon books. And from his reading of the stories of men who had made successes, he acquired not only the ambition to make a like success of himself, but the basic principles on which to build it.

Today, as a monument to his Boll Weevil, there stands a constantly growing, successful business, worth millions, with a vast list of customers that swear by—not at—its founder. And he is still a comparatively young man, healthy, active, putting in eight or ten hours at work every day, an enthusiastic horseman, a lover of all sports.

"There is no handicap, either hereditary or environmental, which cannot be compensated, if you are not afraid to try." Thus wrote one of New York's greatest psychiatrists. "No situation in our heredity or in our environment can compel us to remain unhappy. No situation need discourage one or hold him back from finding a degree of happiness and success."

Age, poverty, ill-health—none of these things can hold back the really determined soul. To him they are merely steppingstones to success—spurs that urge him on to greater things. There is no limit upon you—except the one you put upon yourself.

"Ships sail east, and ships sail west, By the very same breezes that blow; It's the set of the sails, And not the gales, That determine where they go."

Men thought they had silenced John Bunyan when they threw him into prison. But he produced "Pilgrim's Progress" on twisted paper used as a cork for the milk jug.

Men thought that blind Milton was done. But he dictated "Paradise Lost."

Like the revolutionist of whom Tolstoy wrote—"You can imprison my body, but you cannot so much as approach my ideas."

You cannot build walls around a thought. You cannot imprison an idea. You cannot cage the energy, the enthusiasm, the enterprise of an ambitious spirit.

This it is that distinguishes us from the animals. This it is that makes us in very truth Sons of God.

"Waste no tears Upon the blotted record of lost years, But turn the leaf And smile, oh, smile to see The fair, white pages that remain for thee."

—ELLA WHEELER WILCOX

CHAPTER 10

THE UNDYING FIRE

"I want to do one kindly deed each day To help someone to find a better way. I want to lend a hand to one in need Or find some lonely stray that I may feed. I want to sing for someone a loved song To give them courage when the road is long. If just one smile of mine can lighten pain Then I shall feel I have not lived in vain."

—LENA STEARNSBOLTON

IN AN OLD NEWSPAPER CLIPPING, I read of a fire on the hearth of a farmhouse in Missouri that has not been out for a hundred years.

When the builder of that old homestead left Kentucky with his young bride a hundred years ago, he took with him some live coals from the home fireplace, swinging in an iron pot slung from the rear axle of his prairie schooner. Matches were unknown in those days, and the making of fire from flint and steel was too uncertain. So all through the long trek from Kentucky to Missouri, he kept that little fire alive, finally transferring it to his new log cabin home.

There his children grew and prospered. There he lived and there he died—by the light and warmth of that living fire. And so it must be with love—an undying fire.

The ancient Greeks had a legend that all things were created by love. In the beginning, all were happy. Love reigned supreme, and life was everywhere. Then one night while Love slept, Hate came—and everything became discordant, unhappy, dying.

Thereafter, when the sun of Love rose, life was renewed, happiness abounded. But when the night of Hate came, then came discord too, and sorrow and ashes. And truly without love, life would be dead...a thing of wormwood and death.

"I have seen tenderness and pity trace
A line of beauty on a homely face,
And dull and somewhat ordinary eyes
Made brilliant by a flash of glad surprise,
And lips relax and soften happily
At unexpected generosity.
But, oh, what strange, delightful mystery
Is there in love's breath-taking alchemy,
With power to take a drab, gray chrysalis
And form such radiant loveliness as this!"

—OPALW INSTEAD

The most fascinating women in history—Cleopatra, Helen of Troy, Catherine the Great, Queen Elizabeth, the Pompadour—none of them had beautiful features. Cleopatra's nose was much too big—but that didn't keep her from holding the ruler of the then-known world under her thumb for ten long years, and after his death, subjugating Anthony in his turn.

Of course, she had something else—as did all these famous women of history—something stronger, more subtle, more fascinating than beauty. She had charm—that enticing, bewildering thing called feminine charm; the same charm that is born in every daughter of Eve who has the brains to use it.

What is charm? Charm is something in the glance of the eyes, the turn of the head, the touch of the hand, that sends an electric thrill through every fiber of the one at whom it is directed, that speeds up his rate of motion. Charm is taking the gifts that God has given you and keeping them supernally young and fresh and alive. Charm is being so exquisitely buoyant and full of life, *keeping the magnet within you so surcharged with the joy of life*, that even poor features are lost sight of in the bewitching attraction of the whole.

Charm is keeping your loveliness all through life. It is holding on to your ability to stir the pulses and speed up the rate of motion of the one you love.

"For those we love, we venture many things,
The thought of them gives spirit flaming wings,
For those we love, we labor hard and long,
To dream of them stirs in the heart a song.
For those we love, no task can be too great,
We forge ahead, defying adverse fate.
For those we love, we seek Life's highest goal,
And find contentment deep within the soul."

"Though we travel the world over to find the beautiful," wrote Emerson, "we must carry it with us or we find it not." Charm is not to be bought in jars or bottles. Nor is beauty. Both must come from within. Both spring from that magnet of life which is the Creative Force within us.

There are women who seem to have been born tired—never exactly sick, never entirely well. They don't go out because they don't get any fun out of play. They are sallow, listless, having neither charm nor personality, because they have allowed the magnet of life within them to run down. To them I would say—renew your health first, renew your energy and vigor, renew your interest in those around you, speed up your own rate of motion—then begin to look for love. "For love," says Browning, "is energy of life."

"For life, with all it yields of joy or woe
And hope and fear,
Is just our chance of the prize of learning love—
How love might be, hath been indeed, and is."

How to inspire love in another? By first cultivating it in yourself. Love begets love, you know. Charge your mental magnet with thoughts of unselfish love and devotion, give to the loved one in your thoughts the admiration, the appreciation, the idealized service you would like to give in reality—and as you give, love will come back to you.

Love is giving. It cannot be jealous, for it seeks only the good of the one loved.

"Blessed is he that truly loves and seeketh not love in return," said St. Francis of Assisi. "Blessed is he that serves and desires not to be served. Blessed is he that doeth good unto others and seeketh not that others do good unto him."

Love such as that is never lost or wasted. It comes back as surely as the morrow's sun—oftentimes not from the one to whom you sent it, but it comes back, nevertheless, blessed and amplified. As Barrie says—"Those who bring happiness into the lives of others cannot keep it from themselves."

And Ella Wheeler Wilcox wrote—

> *"Who giveth love to all*
> *Pays kindness for unkindness, smiles for frowns*
> *And lends new courage to each fainting heart,*
> *And strengthens hope and scatters joy abroad."*

Why is it that many married women grow old quickly, lose their youthful lines and rounded cheeks, get sallow and wane while their husbands are still in their prime?

Bearing children? There are thousands of women with three and four and five children who still look as youthful as when they married.

Work? A reasonable amount of work is good for every woman. Then what is the reason?

STRAIN—unending, unceasing strain. There is not a servant in this country that you could hire to work every day and all day, without any period of freedom, any day of rest. Yet many men think nothing of making their wives do it.

When Taylor, the great efficiency engineer, was called in to re-organize the work of a certain foundry, he found a number of men with wheel-barrows engaged in carting pig iron from the pile in the yard to the cupola. They worked continuously, without rest except for lunch, and careful checking showed that each man carted from twelve to fifteen tons of pig iron a day. At the end of the day they were worn out.

Taylor took one of the men (an entirely average man), stood over him with a watch, and had him work exactly in accordance with his directions. He would have him load his barrow with pig iron, wheel it over to the cupola, dump it—then sit down and rest, utterly relaxing for a minute or more. When the minute was up, he would go through the same performance—and again rest.

It took two or three days to figure out the best periods of rest, but at the end of the week, Taylor's man was carting forty-five tons of pig iron every day, where before he had carted twelve to fifteen! And at the end of the day he was still fresh, where before he had been worn out.

If you have ever seen an army on the march, you know that no matter how great the hurry, the men are allowed to fall out for five minutes in every hour, and completely relax. Why? Because it has been found that this relaxation and rest enables them to march farther and faster.

There is not an organ in the body that does not require and take its period of rest, from the heart and lungs to the stomach and digestive tracts. Yet many a wife and mother goes all day and every day with never a moment of relaxation, never a minute when her nerves are not taut with strain. Is it any wonder they grow old years before their time? Is it any wonder they are nervous and irritable, unhappy themselves and making those around them depressed and unhappy?

To every such mother, I would say, first—relax. Sit down, lie down, every chance you get—*and just let go!* Don't listen for the baby—don't worry about dinner. Just blissfully relax—even if only for a minute or two at a time. If you can multiply those minutes by a dozen times a day, you will be surprised how much better you feel when night comes.

Give your inner magnet a chance to renew itself. Remember, the first essential toward speeding up your rate of motion is to relax, to get rid of your tensions, to LET the Creative Force work through you. Only then can you draw to you kindred elements of good.

> *"I pray the prayer the Easterns do,*
> *May the peace of God abide with you.*
> *Wherever you stop—wherever you go—*
> *May the beautiful palms of God grow;*
> *Thru days of love and nights of rest*
> *May the love of sweet God make you blest.*
> *I touch my heart as the Easterns do*
> *May the love of God abide with you."*

CHAPTER 11

PRAYER

"But the stars throng out in their glory,
And they sing of the God in man;
They sing of the mighty Master,
Of the loom His fingers span,
Where a star or a soul is part of the whole,
And weft in the wondrous plan."

—ROBERT SERVICE

IF YOU WOULD know the surest way of speeding up your rate of motion, and overtaking the things you desire, try PRAYER!

But when I say "prayer", I don't mean the begging kind. I don't mean a lot of vain repetitions, that seldom have the attention even of the one repeating them, much less of the Lord. Go to the Bible, and you will learn how to pray.

Out of 600,000 words in the Old Testament, only six, when literally translated, mean to "ask for" things in prayer, and each of these six is used but once.

Against that, the word "palal" is used hundreds of times to signify "to pray." And "palal" means— "To judge yourself to be a marvel of creation; to recognize amazing wonders deep within your soul."

Wouldn't that seem to indicate that prayer was meant to be a realization of the powers deep within you? Wouldn't you judge that all you need to do is to expand your consciousness to take in whatever it is that you desire?

"What things soever you ask for when you pray, believe that ye receive them, and ye shall have them." You are not to think of your lacks and needs. You are to visualize the things you want! You are not to worry about this debt or that note, but mentally see the Infinite Supply all about you. "All that you need is near ye, God is complete supply. Trust, have faith, then hear ye, dare to assert the 'I'."

Remember this: If you pray to God, but keep your attention on your problem, you will still have your problem. You'll run into it and continue to run into it as long as you keep your attention focused upon it. What you must do is fix your attention upon God—upon His goodness, His love, His power to remedy any ill or adjust any untoward condition. Focus your attention upon these, and these are the conditions you will run into.

Prayer is expansion, and expansion of yourself into the God-self all around you. As Kahlil Gibran describes it in his great book "The Prophet"—"For what is prayer but the expansion of yourself into the living ether. When you pray, you rise to meet in the air those who are praying at that very hour, and whom save in prayer you may not meet. Therefore let your visit to the temple invisible be for naught save ecstasy and sweet communion. I cannot teach you to pray in words. God listens not to your words save when He Himself utters them through your lips."

Prayer is a realization of your Oneness with God, and of the infinite power this gives you. It is an acceptance of the fact that there is nothing on earth you cannot have—once you have mentally accepted the fact that you CAN have it. Nothing you cannot do—once your mind has grasped the fact that you CAN do it.

Prayer, in short, is thanksgiving for the infinite good God *has* given you. The word most often used for "prayer" in the Bible means—"To sing a song of joy and praise." And see how often you are adjured to "Praise the Lord and be thankful, that THEN shall the earth yield her increase." Probably no life chronicled in the Scriptures was more beset with trials and dangers than that of King David. And what was his remedy? What brought him through all tribulations to power and riches? Just read the Psalms of David and you will see.

"God reigneth; let the earth rejoice;
Let the multitude of isles be glad.
Bless God, O my soul;
And all that is within me, bless his His holy name...
Who forgiveth all thine iniquities;
Who healeth all thy diseases."

Throughout the Bible we are told—"In everything by prayer and supplication WITH THANKSGIVING let your requests be made known unto God." Again and again the root of inspiration and attainment is stressed: Rejoice, be glad, praise, give thanks! "Prove me now herewith, saith the Lord of Hosts, if I will not open you the window of Heaven and pour you out a blessing, that there shall not be room enough to receive it."

The most complete interpretation of prayer I have heard came from the man who wrote—"Once I used to say 'Please.' Now I say, 'Thank you.'" "Enter into His gates with thanksgiving," the Psalmist bade us, "and into His courts with praise. Be thankful unto Him and bless His name."

Someone has said that prayer is the spirit of God pronouncing His works good. "This is the day Jehovah hath made. We will rejoice and be glad in it." It is sound psychology as well, as Prof. Wm. James of Harvard testified. "If you miss the joy," he wrote, "you miss all."

Complete, wholehearted reliance upon God—that is the prayer of faith. Not an imploring of God for some specific thing, but a clear, unquestioning recognition that the power to be and do and have the things you want is inherent in you, that you have only to recognize this power and put your trust in it to get anything of good you wish.

But perhaps you have prayed long and fervently for some particular thing, and it has not come? What then? Has it ever occurred to you that the answer was there, but you didn't receive it because you were not ready or willing to accept it?

God always answers prayer. Over and over He tells us this. The answer to your prayer is as sure as tomorrow's sunrise. YOU are the one who is not sure. You are not sure, and so you do not accept the answer.

If you accepted it, you would act on it, wouldn't you? Did you ever act upon the answer to those long and fervent prayers of yours? Yet that is the way it must be, if you are to pray for an answer— and GET it. If you pray for health, you must accept health. You must act as though you already had it. If you pray for other things, you must accept them at once and start doing—even on the smallest scale—the things you would do when the answer to your prayer became evident.

Dr. Alexis Carrel, the brilliant scientist who for many years headed the Rockefeller Institute, stated that, "prayer is the most powerful form of energy one can generate."

"The influence of prayer on the human mind and body," Dr. Carrel went on to say, "is as demonstrable as that of secreting glands. Its results can be measured in terms of increased physical buoyancy, greater intellectual vigor, moral stamina, and a deeper understanding of the realities underlying human relationships... Prayer is as real as terrestrial gravity. As a physician, I have seen men, after all other therapy had failed, lifted out of disease and melancholy by the serene effort of prayer. It is the only power in the world that seems to overcome the so-called 'laws of nature', the occasions on which prayer has dramatically done this have been termed 'miracles.' But a constant, quieter miracle takes place hourly in the hearts of men and women who have discovered that prayer supplies them with a steady flow of sustaining power in their daily lives."

An old peasant was kneeling alone in a village church, long after the services had ended. "What are you waiting for?" the priest asked him. "I am looking at Him," the peasant replied, "and He is looking at me." That is prayer, of the kind that Emerson said—"No man ever prayed without learning something."

"I never try to do my work by my own power alone.
When I begin I make my prayer before God's holy throne.
I ask that His Almighty power may work its will through me
And so each task is done with ease;
I'm charged with power, you see."

—HANNAH ORTH

Two thousand years before Christ, it was said in the Vedas that if two people would unite their forces, they could conquer the world, though singly they might be powerless. And psychologists and metaphysicians everywhere agree that the power of two minds united in a single cause is not merely their individual powers added together, but multiplied manifold.

Perhaps this can best be explained in terms of electrical power. Take an ordinary magnet capable of lifting, let us say, 10 pounds of iron. Wrap this magnet with wire and charge it with the current from a small battery, it will lift—not merely ten pounds, but a hundred pounds or more!

That is what happens when one person prays and believes, and another adds his prayer and his faith. If you were stuck in a muddy road with a heavily loaded two-horse wagon, and I were stuck with another right behind you, what would be the quickest way out? To unhitch my horses, would it not, couple them on to your wagon tongue and let the two teams pull you out. They could then take my wagon in its turn and pull it onto solid ground. What neither team could accomplish alone, the two pulling together could easily do.

Have you ever noticed a locomotive pulling a long train of cars? To START such a train takes 90% of the locomotive's power. To keep it running on a smooth stretch takes less than 1%. So, a freight locomotive must have nearly a hundred times as much power as it needs for ordinary smooth running.

You are like a locomotive in that. To start you on the road to success requires every bit of energy you can muster. To keep you there, once you have reached the top, needs only a fraction of your abilities. The locomotive must carry its extra 99% of power as a reserve, to start it again when it stops for orders or water or to pick up or unload freight, or to carry it over a heavy grade. It can do nothing with all that extra energy at other times, except blow off steam.

But what about you? You need your full 100% to get started. Probably there are many times when you draw upon all of it to carry you through some grave difficulty, to push aside some obstacle that bars your way. But for the most part, you just carry that extra energy as reserve. What can you do with it? Find outlets for it.

All around you are men and women—earnest, hardworking men and women—who have put their hearts into their work, but lack some of the 100% energy that would start them on the road to success. They are like freight locomotives that are perfect engines, but not quite up to the task of starting as heavy a train as has been given them. Give them a push, help them to get started or over the hump of some obstacle or difficulty, and they will go far. But getting started is too much for them alone.

Why should you do this? Because only thus can you profit from that excess energy you have to carry for emergencies, but which you so seldom use. How do you profit? Through the additional reserve power it brings you. A stalled train is a useless thing. Worse than that, it is an encumbrance, in the way of everything else that uses the line. It may be generating all but 10% of the power required to move it, but without that 10%, the 90% is useless. So the 10% you furnish to get it started is of as much value to it as the 90% it furnishes, and is entitled to as great reward. When you help another in that way, you have in effect grub-staked him, and you share in the spiritual power that his success brings him. As Edwin Markham put it in his little poem—

"There is a destiny that mates us brothers; No man goes his way alone;

All that we send into the lives of others Comes back into our own."

So whenever you have some earnest purpose, or want to help a friend or loved one to accomplish some greatly cherished ambition, unite in prayer for a few minutes each day until you have brought about the answer to that desire.

And when praying alone, remember:

First, center your thoughts *on the thing that you want*—not on your need.

Second, read the 91st and the 23rd Psalms, just as a reminder of God's power and His readiness to help you in all your needs.

Third, *be thankful,* not merely for past favors, *but for granting of this favor you are now asking.* To be able to thank God for it sincerely, in advance of its actual material manifestation, is the finest evidence of belief.

Fourth, BELIEVE! Picture the thing that you want so clearly, see it in your imagination so vividly, that you can actually BELIEVE THAT YOU HAVE IT!

It is this sincere conviction, registered upon your subconscious mind that brings the answer to your prayers. Once convince your subconscious mind that you HAVE the thing that you want, and you can forget it and go on to your next problem. Mind will attend to the rest. So "sing and rejoice" that you HAVE the answer to your prayer. Literally shout for joy, as did the Sons of God in days of old.

Fifth, remember Emerson's advice—"Do the thing and you shall have the power."

Start doing— even on a small scale—whatever it is that you will do when the answer to your prayer is materially evident. In other words, ACCEPT the thing you have asked for! Accept it—and start using it.

> *"If you have faith in God, or man, or self,*
> *Say so; if not, push back upon the shelf*
> *Of silence all your thoughts till faith shall come.*
> *No one will grieve because your lips are dumb."*

—ELLA WHEELER WILCOX

99

BN Publishing

Improving People's Life

www.bnpublishing.com

CPSIA information can be obtained at www.ICGtesting.com
Printed in the USA
BVOW09s1927290115
385605BV00005B/137/P